L A Z Z I

L A Z Z I

The Comic Routines of the Commedia dell'Arte

Mel Gordon

Performing Arts Journal Publications
New York

9 8 7 6

Library of Congress Cataloging in Publication Data
Lazzi: Comic Routines of the Commedia dell'Arte
Library of Congress Catalog Card No.: 83-62613
ISBN: 0-933826-69-9 (paper)

Printed in the United States of America on acid-free paper

PAJ Playscripts General Editors: Bonnie Marranca & Gautam Dasgupta

Publication of this book has been made possible in part by grants received from the National Endowment for the Arts, Washington, D.C., a federal agency, and the New York State Council on the Arts.

A catalog record for this book is available from the British Library.

CONTENTS

ILLUSTRATIONS

ACKNOWLEDGEMENTS

The lack of practical material on the Commedia dell'Arte has hampered a full understanding of that greatly beloved performance mode. Many theatre practitioners and scholars have shared my frustrations. Some of them have gone to wild lengths to help me complete this project, and I owe much to them, especially Claudio Vicentini, whose contribution appears here; Christophe Bourseiller, Herschel Garfein, and Gennaro Turci, who assisted me in unraveling some difficult translations; and Ginnine Cocuzza and Barbara Naomi Cohen Stratyner, who were the initial editors for the Theatre Library Association.

I. Multiple Lazzi Scene from the Commedia in Paris, engraved by François Guerard, circa 1700: "Lazzo of the Chair" (B19); "Lazzo of the Straw" (C08); and "Lazzo of the Chamber- Pot" (F02).

LAZZI

The Comic Routines of the Commedia dell'Arte

II. "Lazzo of the Tooth Extractor" (B01) from the *Recueil Fossard* by L. Vaccaro, Paris, circa 1570.

It would be difficult to think of an historical style that has affected twentieth-century performance more than the Italian Commedia dell'Arte. For avant-garde directors in the 1910s—people like Vsevolod Meyerhold, Nikolai Evreinov, Max Reinhardt, Jacques Copeau, and Gordon Craig—the Commedia, with its reliance on stereotyped characters, masks, broad physical gestures, improvised dialogue and clowning, represented the very theatricality of the theatre. While performing across Europe and elsewhere from 1550 to 1750, often on informal stages and without dramatic texts as such, Commedia troupes developed large audiences composed of all social classes. It was this last feature that made Commedia so attractive to the avant-garde directors. The most popular entertainments of the first part of the twentieth century—motion picture comedy, both silent and sound, and radio comedy—seem closely related to the Commedia. Indeed, it is hard to conjure images of the Commedia without seeing Charlie Chaplin, W. C. Fields, Bert Lahr, the Marx Brothers, Jack Benny, or Laurel and Hardy.

As if in response to this renewed practical interest in Commedia, scholars in the United States, Russia, France, and Britain began to produce studies of the Commedia that are among the most finely detailed works on any acting style—books like Winifred Smith's *The Commedia dell'Arte* (New York, 1912), Constant Mic's *The Commedia dell'Arte* (Petrograd, 1914), P. L. Duchartre's *La Comedie italienne* (Paris, 1925), Cyril Beaumont's *History of Harlequin* (London, 1926), Allardyce Nicoll's *Masks, Mimes, and Miracles* (London, 1931), as well as many others. So, when the Commedia again inspired new kinds of theatre in the early 1960s, much of the avant-garde theatre practitioners' knowledge of it came from these books.

If the reader looks carefully at the rich iconography in those books, he will find drawings, mezzotints, and paintings of perverse sexual play, nudity, vomiting, defecation, and all sorts of activities involving enemas and chamberpots—images of actions that are almost never described in the texts. For instance, in the authoritative Duchartre book where captions accompany most of the pictures, a drawing of the Doctor administering an enema to Arlecchino's exposed buttocks is described as showing an "injection" with a

4

"syringe." In other books, the authors completely ignore this visual documentation. In fact, the Commedia's celebrated *lazzi*, or comic bits, are rarely discussed in more than a couple of paragraphs. Certainly these seldom even refer to the obscene *lazzi* which make up a good portion of the whole. It is as if these scholars, publishing in the early twentieth century, were psychologically or morally inhibited from accurately documenting the Commedia's best-known performance innovation, *lazzi*.

DEFINITION OF LAZZI

From the beginning of Commedia scholarship, there has been a heavy concern with the derivation of the word *lazzi*. Luigi Riccoboni in his *Histoire du Théâtre Italien* . . . (Paris, 1728) wrote that it was a Lombard corruption of the Tuscan word *lacci*, which meant cord or ribbon. The term *lazzi*, Riccoboni reasoned, alluded to the comic business that tied together the performance. Of course, the practical reality was quite different; *lazzi* functioned as independent routines that more often than not interrupted or unraveled the Commedia plots or performance unity. Possibly the metaphor of an extraneous ribbon or the actual use of ropes and ribbons in the comic routines was the origin of the word.

Another, more widely accepted, etymological theory was proposed by A. Valeri in a series of articles published in the 1890s. *Lazzi*, according to Valeri, was only the simple corruption of *l'azione*, or the action, referring to the activities between the plotted scenes. Still other linguistic theories suggest parallels between the word *lazzi* and the Hebrew *latzon*, trick; the Swedish *lat*, gesture; and the Latin *lax*, fraud.

Whatever the origins of the word, the definition of *lazzi* is relatively standard; "We give the name *lazzi* to the actions of Arlecchino or other masked characters when they interrupt a scene by their expressions of terror or by their fooleries," declared Riccoboni. In 1699, Andrea Perrucci simply defined the *lazzo*, a single *lazzi*, as "something foolish, witty, or metaphorical in word or action." Later scholars have described *lazzi* as "stage tricks" or "comic stage business."

Clearly, the word had a multiplicity of meanings, even for the Commedia performers themselves. It co-existed with the Roman expression *trionfi*, triumphs; *azzi*, actions; *burla*, joke; and the French *jeu*, or play. Generally, *lazzi* refers to comic routines that were planned or unplanned and that could be performed in any one of dozens of plays. Put another way, *lazzi* allude to any discrete, or independent, comic and repeatable activity that guaranteed laughs for its participants.

FUNCTION OF LAZZI

Although the *lazzi* were frequently thought of as occurring spontaneously or off-the-cuff, most were rigorously rehearsed and their insertion in performance sometimes preplanned. Constant Mic felt that the use of *lazzi* fell into three categories: 1) when, in fact, they arose out of the scenic occasion—for instance, when the audience became restless or bored during the performance, when the actors tried to comically cover dropped lines or cues, when the performers attempted to inject new and irrelevant amusements at the conclusion of a scene; 2) when the *lazzi* were an expected and welcomed event for the spectators, who came to see the *lazzi* as high points or specialty acts in the performance; and 3) when the *lazzi* were actually written into the Commedia texts as contrived business. [When a *lazzi* became overly extended or integrated into the plot development, it was called a *burla* or *jeu.*]

How the *lazzi* were initiated on the stage seems to be a point of contention among historians, but again the answer may lie in a variety of approaches. Some were obviously used whenever a scene appeared to drag on too long and were totally improvised by one actor. Others, involving stage properties and several actors, had to be intricately preplanned. Some *lazzi* could be instigated by a single performer, forcing his unsuspecting partners to improvise around him.

An example of a *lazzo* being both improvised and contrived can be seen in the *Lazzo of Nightfall*. If, in the middle of a performance, the Commedia manager noticed that the audience, which frequently did not understand Italian, was not responding well, he, in the character of Arlecchino, could begin a monologue, such as "Time flies at the pace of a snail on the floodwater current that has just stopped. Why Midnight, you hourglass thief . . ." This would cue his actors to start setting up the *Lazzo of Nightfall,* where all the actors suddenly pretend that darkness has descended over them. The same *lazzo* with its fixed or semi-fixed routines, of course, could be decided on before the performance began.

SOURCES OF LAZZI

Although several thousand performers enacted Commedia scenarios during its heyday, except for a single manuscript deposited at the library of Perugia, no detailed lists of *lazzi* are extant. Most of what is known of *lazzi* is from descriptions, performers' autobiographical statements, and notations of *lazzi* sequences—sometimes no more than titles—in Commedia plot outlines or scenarios that were posted on the wings of the stage or appeared in the Commedia texts that were intended for publication.

Why the *lazzi* were never made public can be explained in several ways. While the Commedia troupes could not patent their routines, they were not anxious to have their best work copied or read by a theatre-going public. If much of the Commedia was obscene, judging from the visual and fragmented written evidence, then writing down the explicit details could only jeopardize the troupes, who, like many itinerant performers, were sometimes only a step or so ahead of the legal authorities. Finally, it is possible that it never occurred to many Commedia troupes, like so many popular performers, to write out and preserve their *lazzi*.

THE LAZZI COLLECTION

This book is an attempt to collect and organize the available *lazzi* from the period of 1550 to 1750 in Europe. This listing takes well over half of the three or four hundred names of *lazzi* that have come down to us in several hundred scenari and manuscripts and places them in one of twelve categories. Many of the *lazzi,* such as the *Lazzo of the Two-Headed Eagle,* now exist only as a name. Only those *lazzi* that have some definition were included in this anthology. Where several definitions exist I have tried to include most of them.

The *lazzi* collection is intended for both scholars and theatre practitioners, although in some ways it should not be considered a strictly scholarly work. Rather than include exhaustive reference notes on each of the two hundred-odd *lazzi,* I have instead simply described its use, the characters involved with it, and the place and time of its first recorded performance or publication. This has made for a more readable, if somewhat less academically notated, anthology. Those wishing to locate the original source materials will be able to do so by following the book's key.

Only routines that the Commedia performers or historians have called *lazzi* are considered. In some cases, comic stage play that seem not to be *lazzi* at all are included because the Commedia performers themselves considered these examples of *lazzi*. *Lazzi* that have the same name but refer to different comic actions occur in several categories and are indicated by Roman numerals.

Twelve categories were created because I felt the comic appeal of most *lazzi* fell into distinct modes of humor. In most cases, this is quite apparent. In others, however, it is not clear whether the spectator laughs at the *lazzo* for one reason or another, for instance whether because Arlecchino is making a fool of Pantalone, an authority figure, or because Arlecchino is savaging the Latin language. In fitting a *lazzo* into one category rather than another, I have tried to base my decision on the simplest performance logic. Even then the twelve categories: Acrobatic and Mimic Lazzi, Comic Violence/Sadistic Behavior, Food Lazzi, Illogical Lazzi, Stage Properties as Lazzi, Sexual/Scatological Lazzi, Social-Class Rebellion Lazzi, Stage/Life Duality Lazzi, Stupidity/Inappropriate Behavior, Transformation Lazzi, Trickery Lazzi, and Word Play Lazzi are not mutually exclusive.

Appended to the *lazzi* collection are two typical Commedia scenarios, *Pulcinella, the False Prince* and *Pulcinella, the Physician by Force*. Translated for this book by Claudio Vicentini, the texts show the most common use of *lazzi* during the last period of the Commedia dell'Arte.

KEY TO THE LAZZI COLLECTION

The *lazzi* are listed chronologically in each category. *Lazzi* titles that are italicized are the actual names given to them by the Commedia practitioners. *Lazzi* titles in quotes are descriptive names given by later historians. Cities and dates inside the brackets are the places and years in which the *lazzi* were first practiced. Asterisks after the year indicate one of the following documents rather than performance date.

Venice 1611*   Flamino Scala, *Il teatro delle favole rappresentative overo la ricreatione comica, boscareccia e tragica.*

Rome 1618*   Basilio Locatelli, manuscript volume in the Biblioteca Casanatense, Rome.

Rome 1622*	Basilio Locatelli, manuscript volume in the Biblioteca Casanatense, Rome.
Padua 1628*	Pietro Maria Cecchini, *Frutti delle moderne comedie et avisi a chi le recita.*
Paris 1688*	Notes of Giovan Domenico Biancolelli in Bibliotheque de l'Opera, Paris.
Naples 1699*	Andrea Perrucci, *Dell'arte rappresentativa.*
Naples 1700*	Antonio Passanti, editor of two manuscript volumes in Biblioteca Nazionale, Naples.
Perugia 1734*	Adriani di Lucca, *Selva overo zibaldone di concetti comici raccolti dal P. D. Placido.*

Generally, performance use of the *lazzo* precedes its written description by twenty years or more. Inside the *lazzi* descriptions are characters' names in brackets. This refers to the same *lazzo's* performance by those characters in later performances by other troupes.

It should also be noted that these descriptions of the *lazzi* are usually only their barest bones. A *lazzo* related in a single sentence may have been in fact an elaborate five- or ten-minute sketch. An experienced performance imagination should be able to color in the appropriate details.

ACROBATIC AND MIMIC LAZZI

The athleticism and clowning of the Commedia dell'Arte were always among its best known features. Tumbling, stilt walking, handsprings, diving, tightrope balancing were associated with Arlecchino's normal means of locomotion. The sometimes idiotic or ingenuous imitation of animals or objects was likewise related to Arlecchino's childish and optimistic character.

The Acrobatic and Mimic Lazzi, which were highlighted in two Commedia cultures, Scala's Gelosi Company (1568–1604) and the Comedie-Italienne (1661–1688), were dependent on the extreme physical agility of the Arlecchino performer.

A01)   *Lazzi of the Ladder*   [Venice 1611*]
A series of comic routines, generally beginning with Arlecchino [Coviello or Pasquariello] carrying in a ladder. Then any one of the following actions can occur: (a) Arlecchino walks the ladder as if it were a pair of stilts. (b) The ladder keeps slipping when placed against the wall. (c) Suddenly frightened, Pantalone shakes the ladder as Coviello attempts to pick apples. (d) Determined not to let Arlecchino reach the top, Brighella rattles the ladder as the upper half bends back and forth. (e) In a panic, Arlecchino continues to slip off the ladder's rungs as the Captain shouts for him to hurry and drop his love letter in Flaminia's window. (f) The ladder that Arlecchino [or Pasquariello] is climbing bends at the top so that he enters the wrong window. (g) Arlecchino and Trivelino each bring in a ladder and place it against the other, creating a Roman ladder; they form several acrobatic positions, walk on double stilts, and wind up climbing over each other.

A02)   *Lazzi of Falling*   [Venice 1611*]
One of the best known trademarks of the early Commedia, this *lazzi* is often associated with the *Lazzi of the Ladder*. Arlecchino [Coviello or Pulcinella] falls from a high ladder or wall after being shaken off, shot, or gravitationally abandoned. The humor involves Arlecchino's desperate attempts not to fall. This *lazzi* can also refer to Pulcinella's

III. "Lazzo of the Tooth Extractor" (B01) from the *Recueil Fossard* by L. Vaccaro, Paris, circa 1570.

ridiculous falling fits when he tries to run away from danger and Arlecchino's pratfalls over furniture, often into a bathtub.

A03)   *Lazzo of Binding Them*   [Venice 1611*]
Arlecchino and Mezzettino [or Coviello and Bertolino], both
famished, are tied up and bound back-to-back. A bowl of ricotta
cheese is placed at their feet. When one bends down to eat it, he lifts
the other into the air, and vice versa.

A04)   "Lazzo of the Apples"   [Venice 1611*]
Arlecchino and Pedrolino tame a bear by throwing him apples,
which he catches perfectly in his mouth.

A05)   "Lazzo of the Crane"   [Venice 1611*]
A magician transforms Arlecchino into a wild crane. As he pleads
with the magician, Arlecchino notices his neck becoming longer and
longer.

A06)   *Lazzi of the Cat*   [Rome 1622*]
Zanni [or Arlecchino] imitates the actions of a cat, demonstrating
how it hunts for wild birds or how it cleans itself, scratching his ear
with his foot and washing his body with his mouth.

A07)   *Lazzo of the Broccoli*   [Rome 1622*]
Coviello imitates a stalk of broccoli in the fields so birds may come to
peck at him.

A08)   "Lazzo of the Ass"   [Rome 1622*]
Through magic, Pantalone is transformed into an ass. Zanni mounts
him and feeds him leaves from a tree.

A09)   *Lazzi of the Statue* (I)   [Paris 1670]
Arlecchino is brought in as a statue or an automaton. He plays tricks
on the other characters when their backs are turned, always returning to the statue position when they face him.

A10)   *Lazzo of the Dwarf*   [Paris 1674]
When a servant approaches Arlecchino with a curling iron, Arlecchino shrinks his body, imitating the waddle of a dwarf.

A11) *Lazzo of Falling into Unconsciousness* [Paris 1674]
Arlecchino continually falls into a deadly state of unconsciousness, without regard to his surroundings.

A12) *Lazzo of Catching a Flea* [Paris 1674]
Arlecchino, twisting his body into impossible positions and bent backwards with his head between his legs, catches an invisible flea. He celebrates his victory with a series of double back-springs.

A13) "Lazzo of the Foot" [Paris 1685]
Scaramouche boxes the ears of the other characters with his foot.

A14) *Lazzi of the Sack* (I) [Paris 1688*]
As Trivelino throws packages, Arlecchino catches them in a sack. Each time he bags one, Arlecchino falls down.

A15) "Lazzo of Somersaults" [Paris 1688*]
Arlecchino turns himself into a human projectile, executing a series of bounding handsprings or somersaults that catapult him from one character to another.

A16) "Lazzo of Getting Inside" [Paris 1688*]
Arlecchino, standing on the top of a ladder, falls through a window and returns right back through the door in one movement. Convinced that he is inside the house, Arlecchino marvels that his ladder his followed him.

A17) *Lazzo of the Hands Behind the Back* [Paris 1688*]
Arlecchino [or Pulcinella], attempting to hide behind Scaramouche [or Lelio], places his arms around him, making all the hand gestures for him. In this way, Arlecchino torments Scaramouche by slapping his face, pinching his nose, and so forth. Arlecchino and Scaramouche also play the guitar using four hands.

A18) *Lazzo of Falling Asleep* [Paris 1688*]
Lelio [or the Doctor] calls for Arlecchino [or Peppe-Nappa], who does not answer. Finally, Arlecchino replies but with long intervals between each word as if he has fallen asleep. As soon as Lelio drags him in, Arlecchino immediately falls asleep on the floor. Arlecchino stands and again falls asleep in Lelio's arms.

A19)   *Lazzo of Imitating a Dog*   [Paris 1688*]
To frighten Scaramouche, Arlecchino imitates a dog.

A20)   "Lazzo of the Axe-Grinder"   [Paris 1688]
Mezzettino, given a knife by Arlecchino to sharpen, makes all the
movements of a knife-grinder pedaling the wheel of a grindstone and
mimics with his mouth the noises created by the blade and stone.

A21)   "Lazzo of Running Along the Balcony Rail"
                                                 [Paris 1716]
Arlecchino, pursued, or to prove his identity as Arlecchino, leaps
from the stage to the first spectator box and runs around the outer
railing of the three sets of balconies.

A22)   "Lazzo of Spilling No Wine"   [Paris 1717]
Startled, Arlecchino, holding a full glass of wine, executes a complete backward somersault without spilling the wine.

A23)   "Lazzo of the Hatching Egg"   [London 1729]
Arlecchino, hatched from an egg, learns to coordinate each part of
his independently-jointed body.

COMIC VIOLENCE/SADISTIC BEHAVIOR

Set in a world of masters and servants, the Commedia fed upon the comic subjugation and punishment of the innocent or defenseless—the beating of Arlecchino by a jailer who does not know how to count to ten. Conversely, the themes of subconscious, and presumably unintentional, retribution or retaliation run through much of the minor Commedia action. A sleeping Pedrolino bumps into his master, steps on his toes, and once kicked, immediately strikes him in the face, all this in a guiltless, somnambulant state.

The victims of the violent *lazzi* are usually Pantalone and the Captain. This is especially true in the early 1600s, when the Captain was still associated with the Spanish conquerors. In the 1700s, a new character, neither master nor servant, became involved with sadistic or violent *lazzi*; this is the humpbacked Pulcinella, whose sole purpose seemed to be to torment other characters. His puppet outgrowth, Punch, violated all normative standards through his "dropping the baby" routine.

B01)   "Lazzo of the Tooth Extractor"   [Rome 1560]
The Doctor [or Arlecchino disguised as a dentist] fools Pantalone into thinking that rotten teeth are causing his noxious breath. Using oversized or ridiculous tools, the Doctor extracts two or more good teeth from Pantalone's mouth.

B02)   *Lazzi of the Sack* (II)   [Bavaria 1568]
A popular routine where the victim is either secreted or tricked into a cloth sack: (a) Zanni [or Arlecchino] hides in a sack, which the Captain [or Scaramouche] trips over and begins to beat in anger. (b) Hoping to be sneaked into his beloved's house or a room full of riches, the Captain [or Pantalone] is tricked into hiding in a sack; the Captain is then delivered into a pork butcher's hands, whose sounds of delights and knife flourishing frightens the Captain. (c) Several Commedia characters are fooled into hiding in sacks; confused over the others' identities, they alternately attempt to beat and seduce each other.

B03)   "Lazzo of the Shampoo"   [Paris 1577]
Arlecchino attempts to clean Pantalone's hair with an overlarge
rake.

B04)   "Lazzo of the Glassware"   [Paris 1577]
While spying or dancing, Arlecchino tips over his basket of
glassware or dishes, breaking them.

B05)   "Lazzo of the Knock"   [Rome 1580]
Pedrolino, just arising from a sleep, bumps his head into his master,
Cassandro, and then crushes Cassandro's bunioned toes with his
enormous shoes. When Cassandro kicks him, Pedrolino uncon-
sciously responds by striking him in the face.

B06)   "Lazzo of Cleaning Clothes"   [Naples 1610]
When the Doctor complains that the robe that Peppe-Nappa has just
dressed him in is dirty, Peppe-Nappa fetches a bucket of water and a
broom. Peppe-Nappa then washes the Doctor as if he were a dusty
wall.

B07)   "Lazzo of the Innocent By-Stander"   [Venice 1611*]
Arlecchino and Pedrolino meet each other face-to-face and are armed
to the teeth. They heap abuse on each other, relying on others to hold
them back physically. Finally, when the Captain seeks to separate
them, they strike out at each other with the Captain receiving most
of the blows.

B08)   "Lazzo of 'God Give You Joy!'"   [Venice 1611*]
Franceschina jumps on the Captain's back and Pedrolino beats him
with a stick. Once the Captain has fallen to the ground, Franceschina bows to him, saying, "God give you joy, Signor Captain!" and
departs. Pedrolino repeats the phrase and leaves as do all the other
characters who were in hiding. Confused, the Captain bows to the
audience and says, "God give you joy, gentlemen!" and departs.

B09)   *Lazzo of the Cuff*   [Paris 1613]
At the conclusion of an argument, Aurelia is hit by Flaminia, who
exits. Pantalone, who happens to wander by at that moment, is
struck by Aurelia, who then departs. Pantalone then beats the

IV. *Lazzi of the Sack* (B02) from *The Wheat* in the Corsini Mss.,
Rome, circa 1610.

newly-arrived Coviello, who in turn strikes Lelio, who beats Franceschina, who hits Zanni, the last arrival.

B10)   *Lazzo of the Love Message*   [Rome 1618*]
Pulcinella torments one of the lovers by obscuring or delaying the message sent by the beloved. Pulcinella tells a ridiculous parable or asks the lover to choose "ring or letter," "square or round." Or Pulcinella delays the message by sobbing between each word or denying that he can continue relaying the message.

B11)   "Lazzo of Beating His Father"   [Rome 1618*]
The newly-born Zannilet begins beating everyone because he is hungry. By hitting the others, Zanni demonstrates to Zannilet why he should not beat his father.

B12)   "Lazzo of Tripping Up"   [Rome 1622*]
As Zanni and Gratiano bend down to make fun of Lidia, Filandro grabs each one by a leg and drags them off stage.

B13)   "Lazzo of 'To Revive Women!'"   [Rome 1622*]
Arsenio bemoans the "death" of his beloved, Filesia. Trappola enters and suggests to Arsenio that he need not worry, the way to revive women is to pull their hair or twist their arms.

B14)   "Lazzo of the Flogging"   [Rome 1622*]
After mistakenly making love to an old woman, the Captain, in a rage, hoists her on Zanni's back and beats her.

B15)   "Lazzo of Counting"   [Rome 1622*]
Directed to beat Zanni [or Arlecchino] ten times, the Captain [or the Turk] loses count repeatedly. As he flogs Zanni, the Captain counts, "One, two, three. . . . What comes after three?" Zanni shouts, "Ten!" The Captain begins again, "One, two, three, . . . No, four comes after three." He starts the count again.

B16)   *Lazzi of Killing*   [Rome 1622*]
Zanni and Burattino [or Pantalone and Gratiano] decide to kill Pantalone [or The Magician]. To demonstrate to the other how he would kill Pantalone, Zanni says, "You be Pantalone" and he begins to

strangle Burattino. With his last breath, Burattino says, "No, you be Pantalone," and he begins to beat Zanni. This continues in tandem.

B17)   *Lazzi of the Bastonate*   [Naples 1699*]
Whenever a performance seems not to be going well, a Commedia performer pulls out his *bastonate* (stick) and starts beating his partner. The whole performance concludes in a free-for-all.

B18)   *Lazzo of Circumcision*   [Naples 1700*]
Cola [or Pulcinella] in desperate need of money, goes to borrow from the Jews. Informed that there are two rates of interest—a very high one for Gentiles and a lower one for Jews—Cola decides to convert. The Jews gather around Cola then and start to circumcise him.

B19)   "Lazzo of the Chair" (I)   [Paris 1700]
Arlecchino [or Pierrot] pulls the chair away from the Captain just before he is to sit down. Or the Captain's cape is pulled, so the Captain is forced from the chair.

B20)   "Lazzo of the Stones"   [Paris 1716]
While others are speaking, Arlecchino lies on the floor chewing stones, which seemingly break his teeth and cut his throat.

B21)   *Lazzo of Anger*   [Perugia 1734*]
Lelio bows to Pulcinella, who demands to feel Lelio's pulse. When Lelio replies that he is well, Pulcinella explodes, "Why do you come to a physician then! He who looks for a chamber pot, wishes to shit! And he who looks for a physician, wishes to be cured!" When Lelio asks Pulcinella to deliver a message to his patient, the Captain's daughter, Pulcinella screams "What! To ask me, a proto-physician, to deliver a message. What am I, a pimp! A procurer!" Pulcinella repeats this over and over.

B22)   *Lazzo of Fruits and Kisses*   [Perugia 1734*]
Hidden, Coviella imitates the voice of Pulcinella's beloved. When Pulcinella demands "the fruits of love," Coviello bashes him on the head. Pulcinella complains that kisses are "the fruits of love," not punches. But Coviello continues to slap him.

B23)   *Lazzo of the Boy in the Tempest*   [Perugia 1734*]
Coviello meets the father of a boy who was in a shipwreck. Coviello
explains, "The tempest came and the boy went under." "He
drowned?" asks the father. Coviello says yes and continues, "First a
wave, then a tornado hit the boat." The father asks again, "So, he
drowned?" Coviello says no. Thus, keeping him in suspense, Coviello
continues the story, then concludes that the boy was saved.

V. "Lazzo of the Shampoo" (B03) from the *Recueil Fossard* by L. Vaccaro, Paris, circa 1570.

FOOD LAZZI

Most of the Food Lazzi fall into one of two categories—those that exhibit real food, such as the ubiquitous macaroni, and those that mime its presence. Essentially, the *lazzi* with food hark back to an infantile development, where the zanni characters, or infants, are in a constant search for nourishment. In fact, most of the food consumed in *lazzi* are the kind that babies eat. The passionate and messy behavior the zannis demonstrate toward the procurement of food markedly contrasts with other plot developments, such as the higher romantic states of the lovers or even the complicated schemes of the master characters.

C01)   "Lazzo of the Pie"   [Ferrara 1580]
Pantalone searches everywhere for Pedrolino. Finally, Pedrolino's head emerges from a large pie on a banquet table. Pedrolino explains that the cook punished him for wandering into the kitchen by baking him in a pie.

C02)   "Lazzo of Snatching Food from Their Mouths"
                                               [Rome 1610]
Just as Flavia and Emilia are about to eat, a wild man frightens them, snatching the food from their mouths.

C03)   *Lazzo of Kissing the Hand*   [Venice 1611*]
Instructed by the Captain to give a bowl of macaroni to Pedrolino, Arlecchino finds Pedrolino weeping. Accepting the dish, Pedrolino explains that something awful happened to his wife. Pedrolino begins eating and crying. Saddened, Arlecchino also begins to eat the macaroni and cry. Burattino enters and begin to eat and cry as Arlecchino and Pedrolino tell about Pedrolino's wife.

C04)   *Lazzi of Hunger*   [Rome 1622*]
Coviello [Gratiano, Pantalone, Burattino, or Arlecchino] relates how hungry he is after a shipwreck. He demonstrates his hunger by chewing on his shoes or any property on the stage.

C05)　　"Lazzo of the Water and the Wine"　　[Rome 1622*]
Fedelindo discloses the will of his father and his lover, Turchetta,
faints. Coviello goes to fetch water for her. When Turchetta comes to,
Fedelindo faints as he calls for water. At this point Coviello decides
to faint and calls for wine.

C06)　　"Lazzi of the Waiter" (I)　　　　　　[Paris 1673]
Arlecchino becomes a waiter for Don Giovanni [or the Captain]. A
number of different comic routines are created that allow Arlecchino
to eat surreptitiously or engage in ridiculous activity: (a) Arlecchino
rushes in, declaring that the kitchen is on fire; when everyone runs
to put out the fire, Arlecchino calmly sits down at the table and devours as much as he can eat before the customers return. (b) Arlecchino, using a fishing rod, attempts to angle for the roast fowl. (c)
Arlecchino mixes a salad dressing made from vinegar, handfuls of
salt and mustard, and oil from an oil lamp.

C07)　　"Lazzo of the Barber's Water"　　　　[Paris 1688*]
Disguised as a barber, Arlecchino pours the dirty and soapy water
into the Doctor's drinking glass as he shaves him.

C08)　　"Lazzo of the Straw"　　　　　　　[Paris 1690]
While the Captain pours wine into a glass, Arlecchino empties the
glass, using a straw.

C09)　　"Lazzo of the Rope-Macaroni"　　　[Naples 1700*]
Attempting to smuggle a rope into the jail, Pulcinella tries to convince the jailer that the rope is only a long strand of macaroni.

C10)　　*Lazzi of Smell and Fragrance*　　[Naples 1700*]
Pulcinella smells a dish of macaroni and praising its aroma, makes
all kinds of ridiculous analogies about its smell.

C11)　　"Lazzo of the Royal Taster"　　　　[Paris 1713]
The sacrificial king, Arlecchino is treated to a sumptuous banquet.
But just before Arlecchino can feast on each course, the royal Physi-
cian grabs each dish from him, explaining that it causes apoplexy.
Finally, Arlecchino pushes a plate of food into the Doctor's face.

C12)   "Lazzo of Being Brained"   [Paris 1716]
Scaramouche hits Arlecchino so hard on the head that Arlecchino's
brains begin to spurt out. Afraid that he will lose his intelligence,
Arlecchino sits and feasts on his brains.

C13)   "Lazzo of Eating Oneself"   [Paris 1716]
Famished, Arlecchino can find nothing to eat but himself. Starting
with his feet and working up to his knees, thighs, and upper torso,
Arlecchino devours himself.

C14)   *Lazzo of Eating the Fly*   [Paris 1720]
While Scapino is explaining his plan to Flaminia [or the Fairy to Ar-
lecchino], Arlecchino catches an imaginary fly. He tears off the fly's
wings, studies it, and devours it with gusto as if he were eating a
chicken.

C15)   *Lazzo of Eating the Cherries*   [Paris 1722]
While Scapino is speaking, Arlecchino shows his indifference by taking imaginary cherries out of his hat, eating them, and throwing the
pits at Scapino.

C16)   *Lazzo of Eating Fruit*   [London 1750]
Arlecchino shakes an imaginary stalk of currants with his thumb
and fingers. Dropping them into his mouth, Arlecchino chews them
with delight. Next, in comic and detailed fashion, he devours cherries, gooseberries, apples, oranges and peaches.

VI. "Lazzi of the Waiter" (C06) from Molière's *Don Juan* after P. Brissart, engraved by J. Sauve, 1682.

ILLOGICAL LAZZI

The Illogical Lazzi involve a secondary level of intelligence, which is to say a higher degree of stupidity. Their humor lay with a misuse or distortion of simple logic or rationality. Frequently, the comedy works because the offending character, generally Pulcinella, not only thinks has he fooled the others, but suddenly convinces himself of his illogic.

D01) "Lazzo of the Six Fathers" [Paris 1577]
Arlecchino declares that nothing can stop him. After all, he says, "I was begotten by six fathers" and other biological impossibilities.

D02) *Lazzo of Ammazzarsi (or Suicide)* [Rome 1618*]
Pantalone threatens his daughter, Flavia, if she will not marry Gratiano. Unsheathing a knife, Pantalone declares he will give her three chances to change her mind. If she refuses his third demand, then Pantalone will stab himself. He asks three times. Each time Flavia refuses. Pantalone says "If you won't, then I won't either." Zanni takes the knife and threatens that he will kill himself if Flavia still refuses to marry Gratiano. Flavia refuses. Angered, Zanni declares in frustration, "No more will I commit suicide!" and leaves.

D03) *Lazzi of Begging (I)* [Paris 1667]
Arlecchino tips his hat to Cinthio, asking for a handout for an impoverished, mute beggar. Cinthio inquires whether Arlecchino is mute. "Yes, sir," replies Arlecchino. "But how can you be mute, when you just answered my question?" asks Cinthio. Arlecchino explains that it would have shown poor upbringing had he not answered Cinthio's question. Realizing his mistake now, Arlecchino claims that he meant to say that he is deaf, not mute. When Cinthio refutes that claim, Arlecchio explains that in fact he is blind. When Arlecchino ducks Cinthio's jab, Arlecchino claims that he is a lame beggar instead.

D04)   *Lazzo of "There Is No Knowledge!"*   [Naples 1699*]
Pantalone, confused by the strange events and tricks around him,
begins to go crazy, shouting after each bizarre action, "There is no
knowledge!"

D05)   *Lazzo of "To Give This Up Is to Seize This!"*
[Naples 1699*]
Tricked out of his possessions, Pantalone goes around in a manic
fashion, shouting, "To give this up is to seize this!"

D06)   *Lazzi of Faithfulness*   [Naples 1700*]
Pulcinella and Rosetta swear their fidelity to one another using
grotesque and ridiculous oaths of loyalty.

D07)   Lazzo of the Tempest Survived   [Naples 1700]
Coviello describes a story of a ship in a tempest and how he was
saved from it. Pulcinella repeats the story, but in a ridiculous way.
Finally seeing that he is not believed, Pulcinella explains that in the
middle of the storm he went ashore, entered a city, and found a mar-
ketplace. There he bought two bladders, which he affixed to his arms
before returning to the sea. These kept him afloat and thus he saved
himself.

D08)   *Lazzo of the Fresh/Cool Urine*   [Perugia 1734*]
Pulcinella proclaims that all urine is warm. The servant replies that
cool (*fresca*) urine is that which has just been made and is still fresh
(*fresca*). Pulcinella is convinced by her argument.

D09)   *Lazzo of Good Breeding*   [Perugia 1734*]
Pulcinella asks his wife if any man has greeted her on the street.
Good breeding, she replies, demands that she return the compliment,
then she must open door, invite him in and have him sit down. Pulcinella cries out, "Your good breeding has made me a cuckold!"

D10)   *Lazzo of Pulcinella's Birth*   [Perugia 1734*]
Pulcinella explains to Coviello that he was born before his father.
When Coviello says that this is impossible, Pulcinella replies that
while his father was walking in Toledo, he fell and barely missed

being run over by a carriage. A passerby screamed at him, "You must have been born yesterday!" Since this happened a year ago, Pulcinella maintains, that Pulcinella must have been born before his father.

D11)   *Lazzo of the "O"*   [Perugia 1734*]
Coviello asks Pulcinella for the name of his beloved. Pulcinella tells him it begins with an "O," and that he should tried to guess it. Coviello begins, "Orsola, Olympia, Orcana." Then Pulcinella tells him that she is named Rosetta. Coviello complains that her name begins with an "R," not an "O." Pulcinella replies, "I always like to start from after the "O," how about you?"

D12)   *Lazzo of the Three Hunters*   [Perugia 1734*]
Pulcinella tells this story: There were three hunters—one without arms, one without eyes, and one without legs. The one without arms said, "I'll carry the shotgun;" the one without eyes said, "I'll shoot the hare as soon as I see it;" and the third, without legs, said, "I'll run to retrieve it!" They went hunting. The one without hands pointed, "There's the hare!" The one without eyes shot it, and the one without legs ran to recover it. Then, wanting to cook the hare, the three went to a house without a floor, without a door or windows, and without a roof. The one without arms knocked on the door, and the man who was not at home came out and asked them what they wanted. They replied that they needed a cauldron of water. The man who wasn't home brought a cauldron that had no bottom, filled with water, when suddenly who should show up but one who wasn't there, who had no eyes, no arms, and no legs, and took off with the hare.

D13)   *Lazzo of the School of Humanity*   [Perugia 1734*]
Pulcinella announces that his wife or sister runs a school of humanity at his home. That is, she is a prostitute.

D14)   Lazzo of "Have You Eaten?"   [Perugia 1734*]
Gabba and Tristitia come to Pulcinella the Physician to bring him to the Captain's daughter. Pulcinella responds by asking them if they have eaten. They say, yes. Pulcinella repeats the question several times and they beat him.

D15)   *Lazzo of "Put on Your Hat!"*   [Perugia 1734*]
The Captain requests Pulcinella's doctorly skills. The Captain bows and Pulcinella responds by asking him to put on his hat. Realizing that his hat is already on his head, the Captain becomes confused. Pulcinella repeats his command.

D16)   *Lazzo of "I Am Not a Doctor!"*   [Perugia 1734*]
Malizia accuses Pulcinella of not being a doctor. Pulcinella replies that he is not a doctor, as if he was disagreeing with Malizia. This is repeated.

STAGE PROPERTIES AS LAZZI

Stage objects were often employed as trick properties in the Commedia performance. The exploding book, disappearing fruit, moving table, trick optical machine developed into complete *lazzi*. The audience's enjoyment resulted from the magical aspects of the objects as well as the characters' bafflement over mastering their unexpected actions. Here again the zanni characters are victimized subjects of the almost supernatural objects. Even when properties are used as simple subterfuges, they usually backfire in the hands of the zanni characters.

E01)   "Lazzo of the Magic Book"   [Rome 1610]
Pantalone and Coviello obtain the Magician's magic book. They use it to make food appear but after a time flames issue from the book and frighten all the famished characters.

E02)   "Lazzo of the Bladder"   [Rome 1610]
Arlecchino, wearing pig bladders around his waist, falls backwards and bounces back up. When one bursts, he shouts that cannons are annoucing his arrival. [Other zannis have used pig bladders which create a loud noise, in place of the *bastonate*.]

E03)   *Lazzo of the False Arm*   [Venice 1611*]
Using a false or wooden arm, Gratiano [or a thief] allows himself to be held by suspicious characters. When they begin to beat him, he escapes, leaving the bewildered characters with the wooden arm.

E04)   *Lazzo of the Gunshot*   [Venice 1611*]
Cola [or Pedrolino], hired to murder the Captain [or Zanni], fires his gun, but after the smoke clears, his intended victim walks away. Realizing that he forgot to put a bullet in the gun, Cola jumps on it in a rage.

E05)   *Lazzo of the False Bottoms*   [Rome 1618*]
Zanni [Arlecchino or Coviello] hides ropes or tools in pies or trick purses in order to smuggle them into the jail.

VII. *Lazzo of the Zig-Zag* (E08) from *The Go-Between* in the *Greven-broch Album*, Civic Museum, Venice, circa 1700.

E06)   "Lazzo of the Tables"   [Paris 1670]
Just as Pulcinella and Mezzettino are about to indulge in an elaborate feast, the tables suddenly arise and walk away. Or, part of the
table settings arise and chase Arlecchino from the table.

E07)   *Lazzo of Arlecchino's Portrait*   [Paris 1685]
In the flaps behind Arlecchino's portrait, Columbine [or Mezzettino]
places her face.

E08)   *Lazzo of the Zig Zag*   [Paris 1688*]
Arlecchino [or Scaramouche] uses and expanding hinged apparatus
to deliver a letter across the stage, or to pick the Doctor's pocket.

E09)   *Lazzo of Putting the Bell on His Ass*   [Paris 1688*]
Arlecchino breaks into Scaramouche's house at night. To warn himself when Scaramouche awakes, Arlecchino attempts to place a big
bell on Scaramouche's ass.

E10)   *Lazzo of the Disappearing Fruit*   [Naples 1700*]
Coviello and Lattanzio go to grab fruit, which disappears and
changes into water and flames.

E11)   *Lazzo of the Puppet*   [Naples 1700*]
Pascale scares Pulcinella by dangling a marionette before his eyes as
Pulcinella studies the darkness around him.

E12)   *Lazzo of the New World*   [Naples 1700*]
Arlecchino [or Coviello] shows Pantalone [or the Doctor] his magic
lantern or peep-show machine of "The New World." When Pantalone
places his head inside the machine, Arlecchino passes a love-mes-
sage or ring to Celia. This *lazzo* ends with the machine being broken
over Pantalone's head.

SEXUAL/SCATOLOGICAL LAZZI

The Sexual/Scatological Lazzi, the so-called "stage crudities" of the Commedia, were among the most popular routines, although they remain the least analyzed by scholars. The infantile and adolescent aggressions of shit and urine throwing, humiliation through exposure, of mixing food and feces, of placing one's ass in another's face, and the telling of dirty jokes all remain the domain of the zanni characters. Despite the severity of the practical jokes, Arlecchino's intentions seem without undue malice.

F01)   *Lazzo of the Enema*   [Rome 1560]
A widely-performed *lazzo*, this involved one of a number of actions: (a) Thinking the Doctor will pay him the money owed to him, Gratiano has his pulse felt by the Doctor, who attempts to administer an enema. (b) Arlecchino [or the Captain] gives an enema to Pantalone's mule as Pantalone rides it. (c) Analyzing Arlecchino's urine, the Doctor declares that Arlecchino needs an enema, which leaves him pregnant. (d) Held by a servant with his posterior exposed, Pantalone is unwillingly given an enema by Zanni.

F02)   "Lazzo of the Chamber-Pot"   [Bavaria 1568]
The servant-girl [or Franceschina] empties a chamber pot out the window. It hits Pantalone [or the Captain] as he serenades Isabella.

F03)   "Lazzo of Vomit"   [Venice 1611*]
At the beginning of a performance, or just after drinking some of the Doctor's medicine, Arlecchino vomits.

F04)   "Lazzo of the Rising Dagger"   [Florence 1612]
Hearing about the physical perfections of a certain woman, Pantalone's [or the Captain's] dagger begins to rise between his legs.

F05)   "Lazzo of Burying the Urine"   [Rome 1618*]
Told that burying his urine and that of his wife would produce a son, Zanni procures a urinal that contains both liquids. Before spilling it on the soil, Zanni treats the urine as precious fluids.

F06)   *Lazzi of Urinating on Her*   [Rome 1622*]
Seeing Lidia tied to a tree and begging to be released, Zanni and
Gratiano, both drunk, decide to urinate on the nearest tree, which is
the one Lidia is tied to.

F07)   *Lazzi of Water*   [Rome 1622*]
The mistress [or Turchetta] has fainted and the servant-girl cries for
water. Pulcinella [or Coviello] brings her all kinds of water: rosewa-
ter, jasmine water, orange water, mint water, lily water. Finally, he
pisses in a cup and splashes it on his mistress. This revives her, and
he sings the praises of "the water distilled by our rod."

F08)   *Lazzo of Hiding*   [Rome 1622*]
Arlecchino [or Pedrolino] and Isabella [or Columbine] are alone in
her room when knocking is heard. Isabella tells Arlecchino to hide
since that knock can only belong to Pantalone. Finding no place to
hide, Arlecchino is persuaded to become a chair [or a statue]. Throwing a sheet over Arlecchino, whose arms have formed the arms of a
chair, and his knees a seat, Isabella calls in Pantalone. Unheeding of
Isabella's warning, Pantalone sits in the Arlecchino-chair, but jumps
up, citing a pin in the seat. Pantalone assures Isabella that he is fine
since the pin was so small.

F09)   "Lazzo of Pissing on Zanni's Rock"   [Rome 1622*]
Burattino pisses against a rock, from which Zanni appears and embraces Burattino.

F10)   *Lazzo of Looking to Measure Her*   [Rome 1622*]
Coviello [Flavio, Pierrot, or Arlecchino] sees Isabella [or Filli] asleep.
He admires and praises every part of her body, moaning over this
aspect or that. Before she awakes, he mimes making love to her.

F11)   *Lazzo of Spitting*   [Rome 1622*]
This is a simple action that could be used in several ways: (a) Zanni
mistakenly tastes the poison he is to deliver to one of the lovers; to
rid himself of its taste, he continually spits. (b) To avoid answering
any questions, Gratiano [or Pantalone] spits between each word.

F12)   *Lazzo of "Anca Nicola"*   [Paris 1668]
Pulcinella [or Arlecchino] teaches the female characters the song
"Anca Nicola," during which they must raise their skirts three
times. When they ask him the meaning of this, he replies that seeing
the gate open, men will enter it.

F13)   "Lazzo of the Waiter" (II)   [Paris 1673]
Dressed as a waiter, Arlecchino serves all the food, the salad, an
omelette, and so forth, by pulling them out of his breeches. When a
customer complains about a dirty plate, Arlecchino cleans it by rubbing his ass over it. For dessert, Arlecchino puts a plate under his
ass and shits cherries.

F14)   *Lazzi of the Bow* (I)   [Paris 1684]
Lifting his hat, the Doctor bows to Arlecchino. After Arlecchino demands that the Doctor bow lower still, Arlecchino sticks his ass in
the Doctor's nose.

F15)   *Lazzo of Pulse, Urine, and Prescription* [Paris 1688*]
Pulcinella [or Arlecchino] feels the ankle of his patient and announces, "It's a headache!" Then he has the urine of the patient
brought to him in a glass. He drinks it and spits it out (into Pantalone's face). Then, to write a prescription, he has Coviello crouch
on his hands and kness with his ass toward the audience. In this position, Coviello must hold a squid in his anus, which Pulcinella uses
as an inkwell, saying, "Galen, I thank you, ego medicus."

F16)   *Lazzi of the Sack* (III)   [Naples 1700*]
Isabella discovers a sack, which contains the General. Depending on
its hardness, she speculates upon the sack's contents, for instance
wheat or millet.

F17)   "Lazzo of Enlarging the Legs"   [Naples 1700*]
Pulcinella hides under Tartaglia's smock. The movement of Pulcinella's head gives the appearance of Tartaglia's genitals bulging.

F18)   *Lazzo of the Pellegrina*   [Perugia 1734*]
The lovers, supplicating Coviello, fall to their knees. Coviella, bending to speak to one, sticks his ass in the other's face.

F19)   *Lazzo of the Dowry of Pulcinella's Wife*

[Perugia 1734*]

Pulcinella explains that his wife came with the following dowry: a windmill in the back of the house—her ass, a watermill in the front of the house—her ureter, and a forest beneath the house—her pubic hair.

VIII. *Lazzo of the Enema* (F01) from the *Recueil Fossard* by L. Vaccaro, Paris, circa 1570.

SOCIAL-CLASS REBELLION LAZZI

Like the Lazzi of Comic Violence, the Social-Class Rebellion Lazzi are predicated on a universe of unfair socio-economic arrangements. Here, the humor results not so much in the actions of the characters as in their outcomes; the master asks a zanni, especially the cantankerous Pulcinella, to do something and zanni acts upon it in such a way as to not do it at all. Often, the humor grows out of a class reversal, the servant acts like a master and the master becomes confused. Another difference between these *lazzi* and those of the Comic Violence is the conscious level at which these tricks are carried out.

G01)   "Lazzo of 'I Say!'"   [Venice 1611*]
Arlecchino tells Pantalone that from now on everything will be as he says. Burattino follows, telling Pantalone that Arlecchino is wrong, everything will be as he says. Flavio cries to Pantalone that everything should be as he says. Flaminia then tells her father, Pantalone, that she knows everything will be as she says. Pedrolino instructs Pantalone to pay no attention to the others since everything will be as he says. All this leaves Pantalone stupified.

G02))   *Lazzo of Silence*   [Venice 1611*]
Pedrolino [or Pulcinella] becomes dumbfounded when his master shouts at him for doing what Pedrolino thought was a duty that his master had requested. Other characters enter the stage, each with a ridiculous reason for scolding Pedrolino. All this time Pedrolino is silent. When the Captain pinches Pedrolino to see if he is awake, Pedrolino gives out a frightened cry that scares the other characters. Pedrolino calmly exits.

G03)   *Lazzo of "Go Back and Knock!"*   [Rome 1622*]
The Captain takes Pulcinella for a servant in Pulcinella's house. The Captain asks Pulcinella for Pulcinella. Pulcinella replies, "Go back and knock!" The Captain does so. This repeats several times.

G04)   *Lazzi of Rage*   [Rome 1622*]
After being bawled out by the Captain, Zanni and Coviello silently
receive the scolding. As soon as the Captain leaves, they show complete mimic of rage. When the Captain returns, they resume their
first bland attitude.

G05)   *Lazzo of Repitition*   [Florence 1650]
Everything the Isabella says contemptuously to Leandro, Arlecchino
repeats in a ridiculous imitative tone.

G06)   *Lazzo of "Not This, That!"*   [Venice 1660]
Pantalone screams at Arlecchino to hand him his clothing, but no
matter which piece Arlecchino gives him, Pantalone shouts, "Not
this, that!"

G07)   "Lazzo of the Servant's Will"   [Naples 1700*]
Silvio decides to commit suicide. Expecting his servant to follow suit,
he asks Zanni to make out his will.

G08)   *Lazzo of Playing Without Being Seen* [Naples 1700*]
While the Prince and the other characters are exchanging niceties,
Coviello and Pulcinella [or Arlecchino] make fun of them in pan-
tomime.

G09)   *Lazzo of Making Him Lower*   [Naples 1700*]
Pulcinella [or Arlecchino], disguised as an official, signals those bowing to him to bow lower still. Pulcinella forces them to do this until
they fall over.

G10)   *Lazzo of Shut Up*   [Perugia 1734*]
Pulcinella interrupts his master's discourse. Three times his master
tells him "Shut Up!" Later, the master calls Pulcinella, who shouts
back to him, "Shut up!" three times.

G11)   *Lazzo of the Fly*   [Perugia 1734*]
Pulcinella has been ordered to guard his master's house. When his
master returns and asks if there is anyone in the house, Pulcinella
attests, "Not a fly!" But his master enters and finds hordes of people

in his house. He scolds Pulcinella, who replies, "Well, you didn't find a fly, only people."

G12)   *Lazzo of "Your Honor!"*   [Perugia 1734*]
The master calls Coviello, who responds, "Your Honor!" The master then tells Coviello to ready the crystal carriage with the emerald horses and to prepare a lunch of parrot tongues and roast phoenix. Pulcinella marvels at this request and asks Coviello what it means. After describing his master's richness at great length, Coviello then says that since today is a day of charity, the emerald houses cannot wear their bronze coats because the poor people would rip them from their backs, and so on, with one excuse after another, explaining why none of his master's riches can be seen by Pulcinella.

G13)   *Lazzo of the Horses*   [Perugia 1734*]
Having delivered a horse to Coviello, the creditor demands payment. Coviello tells the creditor that he is not going to pay and that he is returning the horse instead. The creditor shouts that he doesn't want the horse back. Pulcinella, standing by, tells the creditor that since he doesn't want the horse back why doesn't he just take Coviello's gold.

G14)   *Lazzo of "Why Don't You?"*   [Rome 1622*]
Coviello is ordered to do something difficult by the Captain, like capture a robber in the dark or enter a cave. Coviello continually replies, "Why don't you?"

G15)   *Lazzo of the Doves*   [Perugia 1734*]
Pulcinella tells his master that when he released the doves from their cages, he instructed them to go directly to the master. So, if they have flown away, it's their fault, not Pulcinella's.

G16)   *Lazzo of the Master*   [Perugia 1734*]
When Coviello [or the servant-girl] gets caned by his master, Pulcinella throws off, "If that were my master, I'd give him a punch, then hit him with a shovel!"

IX. *Lazzo of the Enema* (F01) from *A Third of the Time* in the Corsini Mss., Rome, circa 1610.

STAGE/LIFE DUALITY LAZZI

Among the most curious of comic routines in the Commedia are the *lazzi* that break the seams of the dramatic illusion. Like Aristophanes' *parabasis*, where actors occasionally unmasked themselves during the play, the Stage/Life Duality Lazzi toy with the scenic conventions of the actor-audience relationship. In a sense these *lazzi* offer a critique, albeit in ridicule, of the theater in general as well as the Commedia event itself.

H01)   "Lazzo of the Chase"   [Rome 1610]
With a drawn sword, the Captain chases Coviello. They remain on the stage in a stationary position as they mime running, each slightly out of reach of the other. As they run, each begins to acknowledge the audience's response.

H02)   "Lazzo of Make Believe"   [Rome 1610]
While describing his intense hunger or thirst, Coviello [Arlecchino] takes a piece of bread or a flask of wine out of his pocket and consumes it. He returns to his pathetic monologue.

H03)   *Lazzi of the Echo*   [Rome 1610]
Pantalone [or Pulcinella] finds himself deserted in the wilderness. He discovered an echo and begins to play with it, attempting to make the echo say ridiculous things. Instead of repeating his last sounds however, the echo begins repeating the first words in Pantalone's sentences, which slowly frightens Pantalone.

H04)   "Lazzo of the Interruption"   [Florence 1615]
In the middle of the performance, actors walk into the audience while other actors are speaking on the stage. The off-stage actors begin to shout ridiculous and irrelevant phrases, like, "Be quiet, the hen is laying the egg," or "The pot won't boil."

H05)   "Lazzo of 'This Beautiful City!'"   [Rome 1618*]
Pantalone [or Pulcinella] praises in exaggerated and ridiculous ways

the beauties of the city he has just arrived in. The city where the performance takes place is used as the name of the stage city.

H06)   "Lazzo of the Good/Bad Son"   [Rome 1618*]
Not knowing that there are identical twins in city, characters constantly mistake the good twin with the bad and vice versa. The gift given by the good son, for instance, is hastily taken back by the bad twin, and given again by a perplexed good twin.

H07)   *Lazzo of the Inside*   [Rome 1622*]
To create the illusion of ferociousness, Pulcinella, hidden from the Captain by a door, speaks in several fake voices, such as servants begging Pulcinella not to beat them anymore.

H08)   "Lazzo of Searching"   [Rome 1622*]
The lovers, Clori and Sireno, search for one another. But each time one leaves the stage, the other appears. This is repeated several times.

H09)   "Lazzo of the Dead"   [Naples 1700*]
After Pulcinella is killed and put in a coffin, he pops up several times during the performance to tell the audience not to disturb the dead.

H10)   "Lazzo of the Script"   [Paris 1711]
Arlecchino tells a joke, which doesn't get a laugh from the audience. He tells it again this time more slowly. Receiving no response from the audience, Arlecchino pulls out a script from his sleeve and reads the joke. Again Arlecchino receives no laughs. He tells the audience from now on he will tell his own jokes, not those of the playwright.

H11)   "Lazzo of Getting Through a Brick Wall"
                              [London 1732]
Arlecchino gives the illusion of diving through a brick wall by employing a second identically-dressed Arlecchino.

H12)   "Lazzo of Pissing"   [Naples 1750]
Before the play begins, Pulcinella stands with his back to audience, pissing. His wife enters and tells him that the audience is already there. Pulcinella slowly turns his frightened face to the audience.

STUPIDITY/INAPPROPRIATE BEHAVIOR

Normal human interaction requires a whole range of sophisti-
cated strategies. The Lazzi of Stupidity, or Inappropriate Behavior,
work on a complete violation of those laws. The Doctor insults Pantalone, then requests a favor of him—to sleep with his wife. Presumably, the Doctor becomes confused when an enraged Pantalone refuses him. Sometimes the humor of the *lazzo* involves a kind of double stupidity, where both characters engage in two sets of inappropriate actions, each counter-acting the other.

I01)   *Lazzi of Cowardice*   [Bavaria 1568]
Pantalone and Zanni [or Arlecchino] search for the man who has
beaten them. They practice dueling. But when the Captain appears,
they suddenly forget how to hold their swords in their fright. Pantalone and Zanni attempt to persuade the other to fight, pushing the
other toward the Captain.

I02)   *Lazzo of the Chairs*   [Rome 1610]
Brandino is guarding Ottavio as they both sit in chairs. Attempting
to escape, Ottavio moves his chair slightly. Brandino follows. Ottavio
drags his chair half way across the stage with Brandino in pursuit.
They smile at each other. This continues.

I03)   *Lazzi of the Luggage*   [Rome 1610]
Arriving in the city, the Captain and Burattino both carry heavy
luggage. The Captain asks Burattino if he can hold on to his luggage
for a minute and starts to walk away. Burattino replies that he has
to tie his shoe and gives the Captain all the luggage, who promptly
throws it back at Burattino.

I04)   *Lazzi of Counting Money*   [Rome 1618*]
Zanni divides Pantalone's money in the following way: He counts,
"One for Pantalone, two for me. One for Pantalone, two for me." In
this way the money is evenly divided.

I05)   *Lazzo of Looking Everywhere and Finding Nothing*
[Rome 1618*]
Zanni [or Arlecchino] is asked to find an object or person right in
front of him. Looking everywhere but at that spot, Zanni announces
that it's not there.

I06)   *Lazzo of the Dispute* (I)   [Rome 1622*]
A common routine that revolves around an endless and frequently
pointless argument between two or three characters: (a) Zanni and
Gratiano argue over who should be the first to eat the macaroni, the
one who brought the flour or the one who brought the cheese. (b)
Zanni and Coviello argue over which is the nobler beast, the goat or
the sheep. (c) Clori and Filli argue over whether it is possible to have
love without pain, or whether it is better to love or hunt. Often, each
character will convince the other of the correctness of his views and
the dispute will continued with the situation reversed.

I07)   *Lazzo of Hunting*   [Rome 1622*]
Zanni and Coviello [or Gratiano] prepare for the hunt by imitating
invented animals. Playing the hunter, one of the characters throws a
net over the other, forgetting the game and thinking that he has cap-
tured a beast.

I08)   *Lazzi of Friendship*   [Rome 1622*]
Zanni is hired by Pantalone and Scapino is hired by the Doctor to
fight their old feud. When Zanni and Scapino meet, ready to battle,
they discover that they are long lost friends and embrace and salute
each other to the dismay of Pantalone and the Doctor. *Lazzi* also refers to elaborate and ridiculous embraces and handshakes of Coviello
and Pulcinella when they meet.

I09)   "Lazzo of the Stupid Discovery"   [Padua 1628*]
The Doctor, seizing upon a trivial and well-known fact, pretends that
he has made that discovery, which is of utmost importance.

I10)   "Lazzo of the Insult"   [Padua 1628*]
The Doctor mispronounces Pantalone's name in various insulting
ways and then asks for the sexual favors of his daughter or wife.

I11)   *Lazzi of the Bow* (II)   [Paris 1673]
Arlecchino [or Pulcinella] bows to Pantalone [Malizia, Bianchetta,
or Coviello] each time Pantalone looks at him. To escape Arlecchino's extreme politeness, Pantalone crosses to the other side of the
stage, but Arlecchino continues to bow.

I12)   *Lazzo of Making the Bed*   [Paris 1688*]
Arlecchino and Tartaglia are assigned to make a bed. Seeing wrinkles on the sheets, Tartaglia commands Arlecchino to go under the
covers to investigate. Arlecchino does so and announced that there
are no wrinkles. Seeing the outline of Arlecchino under the sheets,
Tartaglia says that it is worse than ever. They trade positions and
points of view.

I13)   *Lazzi of Touching and Fright*   [Naples 1700*]
Pulcinella enters the stage and tells of the shipwreck he has survived. Coviello enters from the other side of stage and tells the same
story. Seeing each other, they become frightened, thinking that the
other is a ghost. Only after touching each other, do they realize they
are both alive.

I14)   "Lazzo of the Hat"   [Rome 1714]
Peppe-Nappa's master has a hat so large and tall that Peppe-Nappa
needs a ladder to put the hat on his master's head.

I15)   *Lazzi of Sewing and Sticking*   [Perugia 1734*]
While Coviello and Pulcinella are talking, Pulcinella begins to move
away. Coviello, calls him back, saying, "Sew yourself to me!" which
means stay close to me. Pulcinella picks up a needle and thread.
Coviello attempts to explain himself, "Attach yourself to me!" Pulcinella pulls out a long rope. Coviello, becoming angry, warns Pulcinella that he had better take down his words, that is, take them
seriously. Then, as Coviello continues to speak, Pulcinella begins to
grab his words from the air and put them in a cup. When he finishes
speaking, Coviello asks Pulcinella if he has indeed taken down his
words. To prove that he has, Pulcinella uncovers the cup, but finds
nothing.

I16)   *Lazzo of the Pigs*   [Perugia 1734*]
Pulcinella explains that to avoid paying a tax, he hid a pig in his
carriage. When he arrived at the city gate, the tax collectors asked
him what was in the carriage. Pulcinella replied, "That pig of my
master." So they let him go, but the pig cried out, and the tax collectors found it. Pulcinella maintains that the fault wasn't his, but with
the pig who wouldn't be quiet.

I17)   *Lazzo of Paying Homage to All of Their Names*
                                                [Perugia 1734*]
Pulcinella meets a number of characters. In an attempt to ingratiate
himself with them, Pulcinella begins to praise their names in
ridiculously insulting and long-winded fashion.

I18)   *Lazzi of Searching in His Pants and Pockets*
                                                [Perugia 1734*]
Gabba and Tristitia praise Pulcinella, saying, "You're a man filled
with virtue." Confused, Pulcinella looks frantically in his pants and
pockets.

I19)   "Lazzo of the Unanswered Question" [Perugia 1734*]
Gabba and Tristitia ask Pulcinella if the daughter of the Captain is
pregnant. Pulcinella replies, "What are you having for breakfast?"
They repeat their question and Pulcinella repeats his. They ask
again and Pulcinella repeats his reply. Gabba and Tristitia run out
to get sticks and beat him.

I20)   *Lazzi of Putting On and Taking Off Their Hats*
                                                [Perugia 1734*]
Gabba and Tristitia approach Pulcinella. Silently bowing to him,
they continue to put on their hats and take them off according to
Pulcinella's reactions.

I21)   *Lazzi of Delight*   [Perugia 1734*]
Hearing good news, Pulcinella goes into a crazy dance, laughing in a
ridiculous manner, kissing everyone.

TRANSFORMATION LAZZI

The sudden and complete change of personality and emotion fuels the humor of the Transformation *Lazzi*. Greed, fear, anger, envy, recognition, all produce an instantaneous transformation in the Commedia character. The shallowness and transitory nature of human commitments is mocked here.

J01) *Lazzo of the Cuckolds* [Venice 1611*]
Taking his leave of Pantalone and the Doctor, Arlecchino says, "Do what you will, you are still a cuckold!" At first each thinks Arlecchino was referring to the other. Suddenly they realize he might have been talking to himself.

J02) *Lazzi of Nightfall* [Venice 1611*]
This *lazzi* was among the most celebrated of the Commedia. Using candles and lanterns, the characters signified that the scene was taking place at night or in darkness. As total darkness overtook the scene, the characters grope around the street, climb ladders into various houses, falling, bumping into objects and people, discovering what they think are bloody corpses, putting their hands inadvertently down other characters' pants and blouses, mistaking identities and conversations.

J03) *Lazzo of Crying and Laughing* [Rome 1618*]
The old man and his son have tricked each other. The old man cries over the departure of his son, but at the same time, he is laughing in anticipation of sleeping with son's mistress. Thinking of the reverse situation, the son is also laughing and crying.

J04) *Lazzo of Recognition* [Rome 1618*]
Often a concluding *lazzo*, this involves the exaggerated and frantic scene of sudden recognitions between several pairs of characters.

J05) *Lazzo of "Yes" and "No"* [Rome 1618*]
Zanni attempts to play a ruse on another character. When the other

48

character asks a question, Zanni answers yes. But when the ruse is about to be exposed, Zanni suddenly changes his mind about his answer and replies no. This yes and no routine continues through a whole battery of questions.

J06)   *Lazzi of the Nymph*   [Rome 1618*]
To disguise himself, Coviello dresses as a nymph. He practices walking and talking like a woman. He also becomes concerned that men and gods will fall in love with him.

J07)   *Lazzi of Fear (or Terror)*   [Rome 1622*]
Another celebrated *lazzi*, this involves the extreme manifestation of fear, usually as a result of a slow realization of real or bogus danger: (a) Satyrs [or living characters thought to be ghosts] frighten Zanni and Pantalone [Arlecchino, the Doctor, or Trivelino] into extreme hysteria; they run about and knock into each other. (b) Sitting down to mourn the death of his master, Arlecchino doesn't notice that Mario has put his hands beside Arlecchino's and his foot between Arlecchino's feet; counting the number of hands and feet, Arlecchino becomes seized with terror. (c) Scaramouche enters the stage and sits down to play the guitar; Pasquariello noiselessly walks behind him and begins beating the time with a sword on Scaramouche's shoulders, which throws Scaramouche into a tremulous panic. (d) Seeing his master stab the Commander, who dies in agony, Arlecchino, frightened, attempts to run away; in his haste, Arlecchino trips over the dying and grasping body, which causes Arlecchino to be even more frightfully clumsy.

J08)   *Lazzi of Showing Surprise*   [Rome 1622*]
Released from the magic spell, several characters are told of their strange or destructive behavior when under the spell's influence. At first they deny their actions and then show extremely exaggerated manifestations of surprise and revelation.

J09)   *Lazzo of "Hermano Don't Understand You!"*
                                                     [Rome 1622*]
Coviello fools the Captain by having Fedelindo pretend that he only knows Spanish, repeating after every question, "Hermano don't un-

derstand you!" Hoodwinked, the Captain leaves. Now when Coviello compliments Fedelindo on the ruse and asks him to share the money, Fedelindo repeats, "Hermano don't understand you!"

J10)   *Lazzo of Despair (or Suicide)*   [Paris 1684]
Despairing over Columbine's forthcoming marriage, Arlecchino decides to commit suicide. He mimes hanging himself, taking on the roles of the accused and the hangman. He draws a knife on himself but then decides suffocation is a more Arlecchino-like death. He covers his mouth and nose. Discovering the difficulty of self asphyxiation, Arlecchino attempts to tickle himself to death.

J11)   *Lazzi of Day and Night*   [Naples 1700*]
Pulcinella demonstrates the two personalities of his master by contrasting his daily behavior with his nocturnal behavior. Pulcinella switches from one to the other in rapid succession.

J12)   *Lazzo of "Berlich-Berloch"*   [Naples 1700*]
Informed by a wizard that everytime he says "Berlich" the devil will appear and disappear on the word "Berloch," Pulcinella tries out the magic. The devil appears and disappears. Pulcinella begins to repeat the words in rapid succession.

J13)   "Lazzo of Laughter into Tears"   [Paris 1716]
Arlecchino begins to laugh hysterically. Slowly his laughter turns into weeping and tears.

J14)   *Lazzi of Begging* (II)   [Paris 1716]
Arlecchino [Tartaglia or Coviello] pretends to be a beggar. First he begs from passersby with his right hand, as if he were one-handed. Then with the left hand. Later he pretends to be a Spanish beggar, then a German one, and then a French beggar.

J15)   *Lazzo of the Six Hundred Ducats*   [Perugia 1734*]
Pulcinella informs Coviello that he no longer wishes to marry Orazio, but rather Cinzio. Coviello says that Cinzio owes his master six hundred ducats, and as soon as she is married, he will come to collect. Pulcinella decides to marry Orazio.

J16)   *Lazzo of Pulcinella's Impatience*   [Perugia 1734*]
Proving his master wrong, Pulcinella is ordered to leave. At first,
Pulcinella throws down his hat. Ordered by his master to go once
again, Pulcinella throws down his coat. Ordered for a third time,
Pulcinella throws down his stick.

TRICKERY LAZZI

Just as the Commedia scenarios revolved around intrigues and deceptions, many of the *lazzi* were nothing more than stock ruses and tricks. While these *lazzi* rarely furthered the plot, they frequently extablished a division of character type: the eternal schemers like Pulcinella and the eternal dupes like Pantalone and Arlecchino.

K01)   *Lazzi of Bamboozling*   [Bavaria 1576]
Zanni [or Coviello], offering Pantalone [or Pulcinella] the secrets of amorous speech, teaches him a thousand ridiculous sayings. Then, with Coviello egging him on, Pulcinella repeats them to his beloved.

K02)   *Lazzo of the Tart*   [Rome 1610]
Pantalone's wife puts a casket over his head, promising him a tart. As Pantalone bargains, his wife's lover slips out.

K03)   "Lazzo of the Country of Cuccagna" [Venice 1611*]
Two thieves enter to tell Zanni [or Burattino] about a magic land, Cuccagna. As one spins tales about the good life in that land, the other wolfs down Zanni's meal. The second then begins to lament about the difficulties of life as the other eats from Zanni's basket.

K04)   *Lazzo of the Lunatic*   [Venice 1611*]
Oratio [or Pulcinella] pretends that he is mad in order to beat the characters around him or to enjoy his beloved.

K05)   *Lazzi of the Card Game*   [Rome 1618*]
A thief teaches Zanni a new card game. Zanni loses everything since the thief keeps making up new rules as it suits him.

K06)   *Lazzo of Rubbing Up Against Him*   [Rome 1618*]
A thief spies a chain on Zanni and rubs up against him in such a way that he can remove it without Zanni knowing.

K07)   *Lazzo of the Smock*   [Rome 1618*]
Zanni begs the Captain that before his throat is cut he be allowed to
take off his smock lest he soil it. The Captain agrees and after
Zanni's prolonged struggle, the Captain assists him. Finally Zanni
shakes himself free of the smock and the Captain and runs off naked.

K08)   *Lazzo of Tying Their Hands to Sticks*   [Rome 1622*]
Seeing Zanni and Gratiano argue over who should be the first to
sample the macaroni, the shepherd suggests that he measure them
and award the largest portion of food to the largest of them. Zanni
and Gratiano quickly agree, but instead of measuring them, the
shepherd ties their right hands to sticks and departs.

K09)   *Lazzi of Blindfolding*   [Rome 1622*]
Pantalone and Gratiano [or Zanni and Burattino] attempt to seduce
Amarilli [or Filli]. She says that only one lover will please her. She
persuades Pantalone and Gratiano to be blindfolded in order for her
to choose her lover without insulting the other. Amarilli departs.
Coviello and Bertolino [or satyrs] enter and embrace the suitors, pretending that they are Amarilli.

K10)   *Lazzo of the Dropped Coin*   [Rome 1622*]
In order to bring Ruffiana out of her house and deliver a message,
Zanni asks her to help him look for an imaginary gold coin. Looking
for the coin and whispering his message, Zanni manages to fondle
her at the same time.

K11)   *Lazzo of the Multiple Thief*   [Rome 1630]
Pandolfo hands Zanni a gold collar for safe keeping. Watching from
the side, Pulcinella disguises himself as a devil and scares Zanni out
of the collar. Cola, watching from another side of the stage, dresses
as a ghost and frightens Pulcinella out of the prize. Witnessing this
whole scam, Pandolfo and Ubaldo enter, dressed as policemen, and
take the gold collar from Cola.

K12)   *Lazzo of Talking in His Sleep*   [Venice 1650]
In order to fool the other characters, Fichetto pretends to talk in his
sleep.

K13)   *Lazzo of the Shoe*   [Bologna 1658]
The guards have come to arrest Cola [or Pulcinella]. He says that
first he must tie his shoe, and bending down, he grabs one of the
ankles of each of the two guards, trips them up, and runs off.

K14)   "Lazzo of the Living Corpse"   [Paris 1688*]
Arlecchino picks up the supine Trivellino, whom he takes for a
corpse. Arlecchino's sword drops and Trivellino grabs it and strikes
Arlecchino's rear. Arlecchino turns around and Trivellino kicks him
in the ass. Arlecchino falls and gets up, starting again to carry
Trivellino away. He leans Trivellino against the wings of the right
side of the stage. While Arlecchino looks out over the footlights,
Trivellino steals to the other side of the stage and leans against the
wings there in the same position.

K15)   *Lazzo of the Flour*   [Naples 1700*]
As the guards come to take Pulcinella away, he sticks his hands in a
bowl of flour and throws it in their faces. Pulcinella escapes.

K16)   *Lazzo of the Ghost*   [Naples 1700*]
Pulcinella dresses as a ghost to frighten the other characters. But
seeing their frantic reactions, he becomes frightened too.

K17)   *Lazzo of the Goodness of Pulcinella*   [Perugia 1734*]
Pulcinella, overhearing the Captain or some other characters, plot-
ting his murder, enters in disguise and praises himself, saying, "Pulcinella is a witty, straightforward, and good fellow."

K18)   *Lazzo of Paying*   [Perugia 1734*]
The creditor finds Pulcinella and demands payment. Pulcinella says
that he will pay the creditor before the spit dries on the ground. The
creditor is content until Pulcinella explains he will now find a con-
sumptive to keep the ground wet with saliva. Pulcinella departs.

X. *Lazzi of Nightfall* (J02) from *The Trap* in the Corsini Mss., Rome, circa 1610.

XI. *Lazzi of Bamboozling* (K01) from the *Recueil Fossard* by L. Vaccaro, Paris, circa 1570.

WORD PLAY LAZZI

The interplay of dialects, misunderstood words, puns, malapropisms, story telling, and foreign accents were *lazzi* normally peculiar to Southern Italy, especially in the 1700s. There, the speech of the Doctor, German innkeeper, and the Jewish merchant were considered *lazzi* rather than *uscite* and *chiusette*, the stock phrases and prattle of the early Commedia groups. Constant repetition, strange use of language, and insults should also be included in this category.

L01)　　*Lazzo of the Third*　　　　　　　　[Rome 1622*]
The lovers have quarrelled. They call on Pulcinella. The man says to Pulcinella, "Tell her she's an ingrate!" Pulcinella goes to the woman, "He says that he'll grate you!" She replies, "Tell him he's a tyrant (*tiranno*)!" Pulcinella returns to the man and says, "She hopes that you get the plague (*il malanno*)!" He replies, "Tell her she's a barbarian (*barbara*)!" Pulcinella relays, "He says you should shave (*ve facci la barba*)!" The woman tells Pulcinella, "He's disloyal (*disleale*) and he betrayed me (*mi ha tradita*)!" Pulcinella returns to the man, "She said, 'Make a serving dish (*serveale*) of boiling water (*acqua bollita*)." The man replies, "She is a temperamental tyrant (*tiranna stizzosa*)!" Pulcinella tells the woman that for one year the man has found her hairy (*tiene pelosa*).

L02)　　*Lazzo of "I Don't Believe It!"*　　　　[Venice 1630]
Confused by the other characters' reactions to him, not aware that he is being mistaken for his double, Zanni repeats endlessly, "I don't believe it!"

L03)　　*Lazzi of Replying Only By Monosyllables*
　　　　　　　　　　　　　　　　　　　　　　　[Paris 1668]
Weeping, Arlecchino enters the stage. The Doctor and Trivellino question him as to his behavior, but Arlecchino only answers in monosyllables. Or, Arlecchino's master questions him while Arlecchino eats. Concerned about a widow, the master asks increasingly complicated questions about her, while Arlecchino always manages to answer in a monosyllable as he gobbles down the food.

L04)   *Lazzi of the Old Man in Love*   [Rome 1699*]
These are sayings used by the characters to describe Pantalone and
the Doctor:

"Old men are like trees. When they no longer make fruit, they
are cut down by fire."

"He who, being old, wishes to besiege the fortress of love is like
an ancient cannon of leather. After firing the first or second shot, it
must retreat or it will fall apart."

"Old men are like plants. Once they have been bent by old age,
there is no danger that they will straighten out."

"Actually they are exactly like camels that, burdened by the
weight of marriage, can no longer stand up."

"Old bucks and old men are similar because, in old age, their
heads become weighted by horns, and they cannot lift them."

"An old man's love is like quicksilver because even though it
may congeal and solidify, it cannot resist hammer blows."

"What happens to lions happens to old men: when they are sick
with love, they can no longer raise their tails."

L05)   *Lazzo of the Greeting*   [Naples 1700*]
Pulcinella greets the Captain or another character with apparent re-
verence, "Son of Jove, new moon, twice the last name of Alexander!"
Then Pulcinella explains, "The son of Jove is Bacchus. Bacchus is a
goat. The new moon is horned, and the last name of Alexander is
Magno (the Great), which, when taken twice, becomes *magno-
magno*. Thus the whole greeting becomes: '*Manga-Manga becco cor-
nuto!*'" ("Eat it up, eat it up, you horned goat [cuckold]!")

L06   *Lazzo of LaFontaine's Fable*   [Paris 1716]
Using a mixture of French and Italian, Arlecchino tells in a ridicu-
lous and obscene manner the story of La Fontaine's *The Miller, the
Son, and the Ass.*

L07)   *Lazzo of the Other's Name*   [Perugia 1734*]
Malizia, Gabba, and Tristitia meet and joke about each other's
names. Respectively, they mean "malice," "he cheats," and "wicked-
ness."

L08)   *Lazzo of Precipitating*   [Perugia 1734*]
Pulcinella [or Coviello] is asked to perform a favor and is shown
money. He takes the money, saying, "You want me to precipitate [in-
stead of participate]!"

L09)   *Lazzo of the Dispute* (II)   [Perugia 1734*]
Pulcinella tells his master that, having been asked if he wanted to
dispute the charges against him, he answered, "Nolis." His master
tells him that he should have said, "Volo." Defending himself, Pulcinella replies, "How could I fly (*volare*) without wings? Pietro told
me . . ." "What person is that?" interrupts the master, and Pulcinella
answers, "Pietro is first person plural." The master calls Pulcinella a
fool since he should have said, "Pietro is third person singular."
"But," Pulcinella explains, "when Corporal Pietro went with the
guards to Naples, he walked ahead of them. Ergo, Pietro was the
first person, but with the guards he was plural!"

L10)   *Lazzo of the List*   [Perugia 1734*]
The German innkeeper reads from a shopping list. Everything is
mispronounced. So, "four chickens" becomes "four broken pillars."
And so forth.

L11)   *Lazzo of the Smoked Codfish*   [Perugia 1734*]
Speaking in a Neapolitan dialect, Pulcinella says, "The master is always ordering me, 'Go here, go there (*va cca lla*)!' Very well, I've
made a smoked codfish (*baccala*)!"

L12)   *Lazzo of "The Queen" in Latin*   [Perugia 1734*]
Pulcinella, thinking in his Neapolitan dialect, has misunderstood
the Doctor. Vergil's line, "The queen for some time had been pressed
by love" becomes "The queen, being pregnant, twice ate raw saus-
age" in Pulcinella's head.

L13)   *Lazzo of "The Anchor Broke" in Latin*
                                                 [Perugia 1734*]
Pulcinella misunderstands the Doctor's Latin quote from Vergil. The
line "The ship cast anchor by the curved shore" is interpreted by Pul-

cinella as "The anchor broke the bottom of the boat and sent a letter
with a crow."

L14)   *Lazzo of "Rumpe Moras"*   [Perugia 1734*]
Hearing the Doctor say, "Rumpe Moras (Break off or End delay),"
Pulcinella thinks that means, "Your ass hurts."

L15)   *Lazzo of the Knocking*   [Perugia 1734*]
The master tells Pulcinella to knock on the door. Pulcinella asks
what the door has done wrong that it must be hit. The master demands that Pulcinella knock (*bussare*). Pulcinella says that he
doesn't want to make a fool of himself (*abbuffare*). "Knock lightly,"
says the master. Pulcinella barely touches the door. "Now knock
softly (low)." Pulcinella bends down. "Knock loudly (high)!" He
stands up. "Louder!" Pulcinella tries to climb the door. This is repeated with the command "call."

GLOSSARY OF COMMEDIA CHARACTERS

Below is a listing and description of the Commedia characters who appear in the Lazzi routines. Generally, the Commedia characters fell into one of three categories: 1) the serious types—the lovers and servants, those characters who fueled the plots and appeared without masks; 2) the semi-serious types—the Old Men, or the masters, who were intimately involved in the plots, but whose odd qualities put them outside the pale of reality; they often wore masks; and 3) the comic characters—the zannis, the valets, who although involved in the scenario's unraveling, seemed to have an independent comic existence; they almost always appeared masked, or at least heavily made up.

AMARILLI. Lover. The lonely wife of a shepherd.

ARLECCHINO. Zanni. A fool or child-man from Bergamo. Either completely stupid or had the wit and cunning of a seven-year old brat. A master of disguises; extremely agile and acrobatic. Had a deep parrot-like voice. Wore a small grey, felt hat, often with a hare's tail attached, and his celebrated multi-colored patched short waistcoat and breeches. Carried a wooden sword, or slapstick. Wore a black mask with a snub nose.

ARSENIO. Lover. A wealthy, young man.

AURELIA. Lover. Frequently the object of the Captain's lust.

BERTOLINO. Zanni. A friend of Coviello.

BIANCHETTA. Lover. The object of both Coviello's and Pulcinella's attentions.

BRANDINO. Zanni.

BRIGHELLA. Zanni. A violent and cynical libertine who normally became involved in schemes of unlawful seduction and theft. His costume consisted of white trousers and a green-striped jacket. Carried a dagger in his belt, which he sometimes used to poke holes in curtains and wine barrels. Also sported a beard and moustache. Wore a brown mask with a hooked nose and up-turned eyebrows.

BURATTINO. Zanni. A flat-nosed idiot, always in search of food.

CAPTAIN. Old man. A vainglorious and insufferable soldier usually from Spain. Constantly boasted of his victories in war and love, but was always discovered to be a pathetic coward and terrified of women as if under every woman's dress sat a man waiting for him. Wore a huge, plumed hat with a flowing cape and an over-sized sword. Also sported a tiger-cat moustache and spoke with a Castillian accent. Bass voice and flowing movements. Wore a black mask with round eyes and a huge, sometimes malformed, nose.

CASSANDRO. Old Man. A friend of Pantalone from Florence.

CELIA. Lover. The love of the Captain and Doctor.

CINTHIO. Lover. One of Arlecchino's male masters.

CINZIO. Female lover.

CLORI. Lover. Daughter of Gratiano.

COLA. Zanni or Old Man. A ridiculous, acrobatic character from Naples.

COLUMBINE. Servant. The maid of one of the Old Men or the wife of Arlecchino, she was a happy-go-lucky and successful schemer. Intelligent, pretty, small, and skilled in dance and rhetoric, she also exhibited a vulgar but charming interest in sex. Dressed like her mistress or Arlecchino, but always had a small apron.

COVIELLO. Zanni from Naples. His personality is such that he has the musical and acrobatic talents of Arlecchino and the happy-go-lucky pomposity of the Doctor. Wore a white costume with bells and a large-nosed tan task.

DOCTOR. Old Man. A pompous and Latin-spouting scholar from Bologna. His speech is filled with malapropisms and gibberish. Often greedy with members of his family and a great bore to the other characters. Had a pot-belly and dressed from head to toe in black except for a white collar. Had a red spot on his cheek and wore a black semi-mask that only covered his nose.

EMILIA. Lover. A shepherdess, the daughter of a king.

FEDELINDO. Lover. Son of Tartaglia.

FICHETTO. Zanni. A pedantic, but clumsy and restless servant.

FILESIA. Lover. A young Spanish woman.

FILLI. Lover. Daughter of Pantalone.

FLAMINIA. Lover. Daughter of the Doctor or Pantalone. The primary lover interest. Beautiful women with a gift for language.

FLAVIA. Servant or Lover. The wife of Zanni or Pantalone's maid.

FLAVIO. Lover. Frequently the son of the Doctor.

FRANCESCHINA. Servant. Vivacious country wench with a propensity toward comic or grotesque love situations. Sometimes played by a man.

GABBA. Servant. Valet to the miser, Roberto.

GRATIANO. Old Man. Common surname for the Doctor.

ISABELLA. Lover. Beautiful and chaste young woman with an independent will. Highly cultivated. Wore stunning silk dresses, often in an antique Renaissance style with necklaces of gold and pearls.

LATTANZIO. Zanni. Friend of Coviello.

LEANDRO. Lover. Focal point of secondary plot. A young woman.

LELIO. Lover. Leading young man.

LIDIA. Lover. Daughter of Gratiano.

MALIZIA. Servant. Male assistant to Orazio.

MARIO. Lover. Male involved in secondary plot.

MEZZETTINO. Zanni. Elegant valet who combined wise and foolish traits. Sensitive young man. Wore red-striped costume. No mask.

ORATIO. Lover.

ORAZIO. Female lover.

OTTAVIO. Lover.

PANDOLFO. Old Man. Varient of Pantalone type.

PANTALONE. Old Man. A cheap and ridiculously gullible merchant from Venice. A foolish authoritarian figure who attempted to disguise his old age through his tight-fitting Turkish outfit. Although married to a beautiful woman, who often cuckolded him, he chased other women. Rarely successful, he never gave up hope. Wore red breeches, a red vest, and a black ankle-length coat. Carried a ubiquitous handkerchief and a money-pouch slung before his genitals. Wore a dark brown mask with a hooked nose. Was bent over from age.

PASCALE. Zanni. Roman valet.

PASQUARIELLO. Old Man or Servant. A schemer, he carried a sword. Wore a long-nosed mask.

PEDROLINO. Zanni. Generally a likeable simple character who sometimes imitated the Captain. Energetic, he pretended to be mute. No mask.

PEPPE-NAPPA. Zanni. A Sicilian valet who dressed like Pierrot only in blue. Performed with swift, double-jointed movements. No mask.

PIERROT. Zanni. A sad and mute character who suffered from unrequited love. Although sentimental, he was able to execute sudden, acrobatic turns. Dressed in a white, loose-fitting outfit with a large collar. White-faced without a mask.

PULCINELLA. Zanni. A misshapen and pot-bellied rascal who combined empty-headed folly and cruelty. Without any morals or scruples, he often concocted outrageous schemes to satisfy his animal-like lust and gluttony. Often hunchbacked, he was known for his bizarrely-paced, bentover, cock-like gait and henlike voice. Sometimes he wore a conical hat and a broken-nose mask.

ROSETTA. Servant. A maid or the wife of Pulcinella. Wore Arlecchino-like, patched dress.

RUFFIANA. Old Woman. A gossip or go-between who wore a mask.

SCAPINO. Zanni. A schemer similar to Brighella. Very musical. Dressed in a rakish fashion with green and white stripes. Wore a hooked-nose mask.

SCARAMOUCHE. Zanni. A lover of wine and women from Naples. A braggart and quarreler similar to the Captain. Possessed of a good voice and was an excellent mime. Dressed in black. No mask.

SILVIO. Old Man.

SIRENO. Lover. Pantalone's son.

TARTAGLIA. Old Man or Servant. A ridiculous old man from Naples. Was a stammerer. Wore thick glasses and a black hat.

TRAPPOLA. Zanni. The Captain's valet.

TRISTITIA. Servant. An assistant to the miser, Roberto.

TRIVELINO. Zanni. A rival, or companion, to Arlecchino. Dressed like Arlecchino.

TURCHETTA. Lover. A female slave.

UBALDO. Old Man.

ZANNI. Zanni. The generic name for the comic servant.

ZANNILET. Zanni's new born child.

XII. *Lazzo of the New World* (E12) from *Pantalone Cheated by Arlec-chino* by G. Zocchi, Paris, circa 1740.

PULCINELLA, THE FALSE PRINCE

*from the Collection of Adriani di Lucca in
the library of Perugia, 1734*

translated by Claudio Vicentini

XIII. *Lazzi of Falling* (A02) from *The Garden* in the Corsini Mss.,
Rome, circa 1610.

ACT ONE

Scene One: Coviello and Pulcinella. (Rooms.)
Coviello and Pulcinella enter, quarreling. Pulcinella complains that Coviello, the maitre d'hotel, gave him a soup so thin that he had to drink it with a straw. And instead of cheese, he served him a piece of soap, and other *lazzi*. They make peace. At this point. . . .

Scene Two: Prince and the same. (Upstage.)
The Prince orders Coviello to call for the Doctor, and orders Pulcinella to call for Ormondo, the first counsellor. The Prince speaks of his departure and says that he wants to leave the necessary orders.

Scene Three: Doctor, Ormondo, and the same.
The Doctor and Ormondo enter and bow. The Prince greets them and makes them sit down. Far away, Coviello and Pulcinella have their *lazzi of bowing* (F14). The Prince explains that he has been invited to a tournament. His attendants advise him to go. Meanwhile, Coviello and Pulcinella have their *lazzi of playing without being seen* (G08). The Prince appoints Ormondo, the Governor; the Doctor, First Counsellor; Coviello, the Jailer; and Pulcinella, the Gardener. They all exit.

Scene Four: Rosetta. (Rooms.)
Rosetta wants to go to court in order to find Pulcinella, her husband. He has not been home for two days and has not brought her any food. At this point. . . .

Scene Five: The Doctor and the same.
The Doctor muses about his new appointment and how it will be useful to gain Rosetta's love. He sees her, greets her, and tells her about his good fortune. Rosetta congratulates him and shows him her oil, wheat, and wine. At this point. . . .

Scene Six: Pulcinella and the same.
Pulcinella says, in an aside, "The fox is in the vineyard." He stands beside the Doctor in such a way that Rosetta can see him but the

Doctor cannot. Pulcinella whispers to Rosetta, "If I find you two together one more time, I'll fix you!" Pulcinella exits. Rosetta warns
the Doctor that her husband saw them together. The Doctor tells her
not to be afraid. After all, he is now the First Secretary; he will keep
Pulcinella away. Pulcinella returns, finds them together, and says in
an aside, "The cuckold is chatting with my wife. If I find them together again, I'll really take care of him!" The Doctor and Rosetta
speak to each other in a low voice. Pulcinella exits and returns with
a stick (B17). Rosetta runs away, as Pulcinella beats the Doctor, who
shouts for the police. At this point. . . .

Scene Seven: Two Policemen, Coviello, and the same.
The Doctor orders the incarceration of Pulcinella by the two police-
men. Pulcinella screams that he had the best reason for beating the
Doctor. They all exit.

Scene Eight: Rosetta. (Town.)
Rosetta frets that Pulcinella may now beat her after seeing her with
the Doctor.

Scene Nine: Pulcinella and the same. (Prison, a cage of five-foot fencing upstage.)
Pulcinella sings a song to Rosetta, "Love has published a decree."
The song explains that Rosetta should be tied to a donkey and whip-
ped, except that she would enjoy it too much. Then Pulcinella complains that he is in jail because of Rosetta. Rosetta reprimands him,
saying that she was only congratulating the Doctor. Pulcinella asks
Rosetta if she would betray her husband for one hundred scudi.
Rosetta answers, "No." For two hundred scudi? "No." For three
hundred scudi? Rosetta thinks. Pulcinella admits that for that much
money he would break his own neck. Pulcinella asks Rosetta if she
will go to the Princess for him and beg for mercy. Rosetta agrees. All
exit.

Scene Ten: Governor and the Doctor. (Hall.)
Seated in two chairs before a small table, the Doctor complains to
Ormondo about Pulcinella's rudeness. The Doctor has sent for Pul-
cinella and Ormondo agrees to interrogate him. At this point. . . .

Scene Eleven: Pulcinella, Policemen, and the same.
Here Ormondo's interrogation begins as the Doctor transcribes the
conversation. Ormondo asks Pulcinella if he has carried forbidden
arms, sidearms, or firearms. Pulcinella answers, "Yes." The Doctor
repeats the question in ridiculous Latin, "Interrogatus respon-
dit . . . Questioned, he answered. . . ." Ormondo asks if Pulcinella injured anyone with those arms. Pulcinella answers, "Yes." The Doctor
repeats the dialogue in Latin. Ormondo asks Pulcinella what arms
did he use. Pulcinella replies, "Grills, knives, baking-pans, frying
pans; all the sidearms and firearms of the kitchen. Everything that
injured fish, capons, chickens, and pigeons." Ormondo repeats that
Pulcinella must "pay, pay, pay" for this. Ormondo asks Pulcinella if
he has killed anyone. Pulcinella replies, "Yes." The Doctor repeats in
Latin. Ormondo asks Pulcinella whether the victim was male or
female. Pulcinella says that he did not pay attention to that. Ormondo asks who the victim was. Pulcinella replies, "Lice, roaches,
and fleas." Ormondo demands that Pulcinella "pay, pay, pay." Ormondo orders the Doctor to complete the decree to banish Pulcinella,
which they hand him. The upstage area is closed as all but Pulcinella exit. At this point. . . .

Scene Twelve: Brunetto and the same.
Pulcinella tells Brunetto that he has just been freed from jail without any punishment, that he has been given a favorable decree.
Brunetto congratulates him and Pulcinella shows Brunetto the decree. Brunetto reads the ridiculous Latin. It translates something
like, "We exile and order that within three hours goes out of this
town, one said Pulcinella Stupido of Cerra, under the threat of capital
punishment. Signed Ormondo, Governor, and Doctor Cocozza, First
Counsellor." Brunetto explains to Pulcinella that the document is a
ban. Pulcinella becomes afraid and begs Brunetto to help him.
Brunetto does not know what to do and exhorts Pulcinella to leave
lest he should pay with his head. Pulcinella begs Brunetto for some
money. Brunetto refuses, saying that he has none. Pulcinella de-
spairs. Finally, Brunetto gives Pulcinella his ring, ordering him to
sell it and keep the money. Pulcinella thanks him and leaves. At this
point. . . .

Scene Thirteen: The Princess and the same.
The Princess asks Brunetto how he likes the town and court, whether he has fallen in love with anyone. She begs him to reciprocate her love. Brunetto refuses, then changes his mind. They engage in a love dialogue. Now happy, the Princess exits. Brunetto muses that long ago he fell in love with the Princess by hearing about her; he then came to the court disguised as a page to see and watch her. In reality, he is the Prince of Greta. Brunetto gives thanks to Love and exits.

Scene Fourteen: Pulcinella.
Pulcinella enters with his bundle: a stick, a bottle, and a pumpkin. He sings, "Farewell to Home." Pulcinella then complains about his banishment. He walks to a forest but suddenly becomes afraid some creature will swallow him. Pulcinella becomes terrified since there is no one around. He calls out and an echo repeats his last word. Pulcinella tries to fool the echo, speaking quickly and playing word games (H03). Instead of repeating the last word in Pulcinella's calls, however, the echo starts to repeat the first word. At this point. . . .

Scene Fifteen: The Wizard and the same.
Pulcinella sees the Wizard, becomes frightened and falls. He makes the *lazzo of falling* (A02) three times. The Wizard then comforts him and encourages him, explaining the reason he has been banished. The Wizard tells Pulcinella that he wishes to give Pulcinella the appearance of the Prince. But Pulcinella does not want to "lose Pulcinella." The Wizard promises that he will make him both Prince and Pulcinella. First Pulcinella must agree to be good to everyone and evil to none. Pulcinella agrees. The Wizard waves a wand in the air. At this point. . . .

Scene Sixteen: The Devil and the same.
Pulcinella sees the Devil, becomes frightened, and falls three times. The Wizard orders the Devil to bring him the "Eo-Meo-Teo." The Devil exits. The Wizard dresses Pulcinella and gives him a magic root that if placed on the real Prince will give him the appearance of Pulcinella. The Wizard also tells Pulcinella a secret: every time he wants the Devil to appear, he should say, "Berlich." When he wants the Devil to go, he should say "Berloch" and the Devil will leave. The

Wizard returns to his cave. Pulcinella makes the *lazzo of Berlich-Berloch* (J12) with the Devil. He demands the Devil wear shoes. Finally, he forces the Devil to carry him on the Devil's back, like a horse. They exit with Pulcinella singing.

ACT TWO

Scene One: Governor and the Doctor. (Rooms.)
The Governor and the Doctor are astonished that the Prince is returning without giving any prior notice.

Scene Two: Pulcinella and the same. (Upstage.)
The Governor and the Doctor bow to Pulcinella, thinking that he is the Prince. They ask the reason of his return. Pulcinella-Prince replies, "Because of their use of justice." They explain that they were acting according to the law. Pulcinella-Prince asks, "Where's Pulcinella?" They explain that he is in exile. Pulcinella-Prince demands to know the reason. They explain that Pulcinella abused everyone and beat the Doctor. Pulcinella-Prince says that the Doctor deserved it, that Pulcinella is an honorable man, that they, the depraved ones, have exiled Pulcinella in order to enjoy his wife. Pulcinella-Prince shouts for Coviello.

Scene Three: Coviello, Policemen, and the same.
Coviello enters. Pulcinella-Prince orders Ormondo and the Doctor to be thrown in jail. Coviello calls for the policemen, who with Ormondo, the Doctor, and Coviello march off to jail. At this point. . . .

Scene Four: Brunetto and the same.
Brunetto welcomes Pulcinella-Prince as the Prince. Pulcinella, in an aside decides to help Brunetto since he gave Pulcinella his ring. Pulcinella-Prince asks Brunetto if he is married. "No." Pulcinella-Prince asks Brunetto if he is in love. "Yes." Pulcinella-Prince asks with whom. "I cannot tell that." Pulcinella-Prince asks Brunetto to make a plate of macaroni. Brunetto laughs. They exit.

Scene Five: Prince. (Town.)
The Prince is astonished that none of his courtiers have come to meet him. At this point. . . .

Scene Six: Ormondo and the Doctor and the same. (Prison.)
The Prince sees Ormondo and the Doctor in jail, complaining. The
Prince asks them who sent them to jail. They reply, "Your High-
ness." The Prince is astonished and calls the jailer.

Scene Seven: Coviello and the same.
The Prince orders Coviello to release Ormondo and the Doctor. They
all exit.

Scene Eight: Pulcinella.
Pulcinella is overjoyed to be a prince. He has revenged himself on
the Doctor and Ormondo. He is hungry and does not know if
Brunetto has made the macaroni. At this point. . . .

Scene Nine: Rosetta and the same.
Rosetta pleads to Pulcinella-Prince to free Pulcinella from the ban.
Pulcinella-Prince makes passes at her. Rosetta protests that she is
not worthy to look at him. They have their *lazzi*. Rosetta says that
she wants her husband. Pulcinella-Prince asks her to face away. Pulcinella removes the "Eo-Meo-Teo" and calls her. Rosetta embraces
Pulcinella. They make the *lazzi of faithfulness* (D06). Pulcinella then
says that he is afraid that the policemen will find him. He asks
Rosetta to look if anyone is coming. When she turns, Pulcinella puts
on the "Eo-Meo-Teo" again. Rosetta thanks Pulcinella-Prince and
begs him for mercy to Pulcinella. Pulcinella-Prince agrees and
Rosetta exits. At this point. . . .

Scene Ten: Page [or Brunetto] and the same.
The Page enters, announcing that the Teacher of Music has come.
Pulcinella-Prince asks what the Teacher wants. "To give the lesson,"
the Page replies and exits. Pulcinella thinks the situation is ridiculous. At this point. . . .

Scene Eleven: The Teacher of Music and the same.
The Teacher enters and gives Pulcinella-Prince the score. Pulcinella-
Prince sings out of tune. He has his *lazzi*. Then they sing a duet or, if
the Teacher cannot sing, Pulcinella sings an arietta. The Teacher
exits. At this point. . . .

Scene Twelve: Brunetto and the same.
Brunetto enters and announces that the Dance Teacher has come.
Pulcinella Prince as before. Brunetto goes out to call the Dance
Teacher. Pulcinella wonders that princes dance and sing, but the
cook never comes.

Scene Thirteen: Dance Teacher and the same.
The scene as before. Pulcinella-Prince practices ballet and has his
lazzi. He falls and chases the Dance Teacher out. At this point. . . .

Scene Fourteen: Brunetto and the same.
Brunetto enters and announces that the Fencing Master has arrived.
Pulcinella-Prince, in an aside, muses that they are going to kill him.
Brunetto exits in order to usher in the Fencing Master.

Scene Fifteen: Fencing Master and the same.
The Fencing Master enters with two swords. Pulcinella-Prince plays
the *lazzo of making him lower* (G09). The Fencing-Master falls three
times. Pulcinella-Prince announces that he is going to shit on him
and attacks the Fencing Master with a sword. The Fencing Master
runs out. At this point. . . .

Scene Sixteen: Ormondo, the Doctor, and the same.
Ormondo and the Doctor thank Pulcinella-Prince for releasing them
from jail. Pulcinella-Prince becomes confused and calls for Coviello.

Scene Seventeen: Coviello and the same.
Pulcinella-Prince asks Coviello why he released Ormondo and the
Doctor. Coviello replies that he, the Prince, demanded it. Pulcinella-
Prince explains that he was drunk then and they must be re-incar-
cerated. Coviello exits with Ormondo and the Doctor. Pulcinella
realizes that the actual Prince has returned and that he must be
careful. Suddenly Pulcinella remembers that he is hungry and has
not eaten. At this point. . . .

Scene Eighteen: Barba Nicolo and the same.
Barba Nicolo enters with a plate. Pulcinella-Prince sees him and inquires what he is carrying. Barba Nicolo explains that it is a plate of

macaroni for the prisoners. Pulcinella-Prince says okay, then calls
him back, saying he must inspect the plate for any contraband. Pulcinella has his *lazzi of smell and fragrance* (C10). Afterwards he tells
Barba Nicolo to leave, then calls him back. Pulcinella-Prince checks
under the macaroni for hidden weapons. Looking at the macaroni,
Pulcinella-Prince orders Barba Nicolo to kneel on his hands and
knees. Pulcinella-Prince sits on Barba Nicolo's back, sets the plate of
macaroni on his shoulders, and eats. Then Pulcinella-Prince breaks
the dish on Barba Nicolo's head, who screams and runs away. Pulcinella falls down.

ACT THREE

Scene One: The Prince and Coviello.
Coviello greets the Prince and gives him letters from his jailed coun-
sellors. The Prince is astonished over these unusual happenings. The
Prince decides to visit his attendants in person. He leaves with
Coviello.

Scene Two: Pulcinella.
Pulcinella muses that had not Barba Nicolo brought in the macaroni, he might have died of starvation. Pulcinella also relishes the
predicament of his enemies, planning to send Ormondo and the Doctor into exile. At this point. . . .

Scene Three: Coviello and the same.
Coviello tells Pulcinella-Prince that he has some legal rulings to ad-
judicate. Pulcinella-Prince asks what they are. Coviello reads the
first: a man driving a cart has accidently run over a child. Pulcinella-Prince decrees that the man live with the mother until she
has another child. Coviello replies that that ruling seems wrong to
him. Pulcinella-Prince calls Coviello an animal. Coviello reads the
second legal problem: there is a heap of debris at the city's gate that
obstructs the way. Pulcinella-Prince declares the debris should be
put in a ditch. Coviello asks about the debris that sticks out of the
ditch. Pulcinella-Prince explains a second ditch be dug for that, until
there are seven ditches. Pulcinella-Prince begins shouting to
Coviello, "Make a ditch, make a ditch, make a ditch." Coviello exits.

Scene Four: The Prince and the same.
Pulcinella sees the Prince entering and hides behind him. Pulcinella then puts the magic root in the Prince's pocket. The Prince sees Pulcinella-Prince and is astonished at his likeness to himself. Pulcinella-Prince calls Coviello.

Scene Five: Coviello and the same.
Coviello enters. Pulcinella-Prince asks Coviello who the Prince is. Coviello answers that is Pulcinella Stupido. Pulcinella-Prince orders the Prince be sent to jail. Coviello calls the policemen.

Scene Six: The Policemen and the same.
Coviello orders the Prince's imprisonment. The policemen start to carry out his order when the Prince tries to pull out his sword. They tie him up. Pulcinella-Prince, afraid, steps backwards and shouts. At this point. . . .

Scene Seven: Ormondo, the Doctor, and the same.
Pulcinella-Prince sees Ormondo and the Doctor and asks who ordered their release. Coviello answers that it was he, the Prince, who ordered it. In an aside, Pulcinella says that they will pay for this. Then Pulcinella-Prince declares that Pulcinella (really the Prince) has disobeyed his order to remain in exile and attempted to draw his sword. For this he must be hanged. At this point. . . .

Scene Eight: Brunetto and the same.
Brunetto asks why Pulcinella must be hanged. Pulcinella-Prince explains and Brunetto begs for mercy for Pulcinella. Pulcinella-Prince refuses. At this point. . . .

Scene Nine: The Princess and the same.
The Princess also pleads for Pulcinella's life. Pulcinella-Prince holds firm. Coviello says that the hang-man is gone. Pulcinella-Prince will do it himself. A Policeman goes to find a ladder and returns with one. At this point. . . .

Scene Ten: Wizard and the same.
The Wizard tells Pulcinella-Prince to stop. In his fright, Pulcinella

falls from the ladder, shouting that the ruse is up (A01). The Wizard forces them to free the Prince and take the magic root out of his pocket. The Prince's sword is returned to him and everyone recognizes him again. The Wizard makes them take the "Eo-Meo-Teo" away from Pulcinella. Everyone congratulates the Prince. The Wizard explains how Pulcinella, having been unjustly exiled, had been forced to take the Prince's appearance and was forbidden to do evil to anyone. Since Pulcinella disobeyed that edict, he has fallen. The Wizard discloses that Brunetto is secretly the Prince of Greta and in love with the Princess. The Prince offers the hand of the Princess to Brunetto. Brunetto thanks the Prince, accepting the invitation and marries her. At this point. . . .

Scene Eleven: Rosetta and the same.
Rosetta throws herself at the Prince's feet and begs for mercy for Pulcinella. Brunetto does the same. Then the Princess. The counsellors screm that Pulcinella must be punished. The Wizard pleads for mercy since he claims Pulcinella is a simple man and did not act out of malice. The Prince promises mercy. Pulcinella ends the play, saying, "Many who believe that they are real princes, find themselves to be false princes." Everyone shouts, "Long live the False Prince!"

PULCINELLA, THE PHYSICIAN BY FORCE

*from the Collection of Adriani di Lucca in
the library of Perugia, 1734*

translated by Claudio Vicentini

ACT ONE

Scene One: Pulcinella and Malizia.
Pulcinella with fur coat, broken stick, and basket. He enters with Malizia.
Pulcinella accuses him of stealing from the master's farm and wasting everything on women. *Their lazzi.* Pulcinella wants to tell the master everything. Noticing the master, Pulcinella says, *"Lupus in fabula."* [Latin for "When you speak of him, he appears."]

Scene Two: The same and Orazio.
After the *lazzi of greeting* (L05), Pulcinella starts to tell the master about Malizia's theft. Malizia interrupts him, saying, "As you ordered me!" Pulcinella explains, "For instance, the other day, Malizia took a basket of apples." Malizia answers that half were consumed at the table; the rest is in the pantry. Pulcinella tells of two quarts of missing beans. Malizia answers that Pulcinella is not aware of their actual tiny cost. Pulcinella tells of a missing half basket of apricots. Malizia explains that Pulcinella is right; the apricots were sown in the ground. Annoyed, Orazio orders Pulcinella to go. The *lazzo of Pulcinella's impatience* (J16).

Scene Three: Orazio and Malizia.
Orazio reveals his love for Lisetta; he must speak with her and orders Malizia to knock at her door, which he does.

Scene Four: Lisette and the same.
Lisette and Orazio have their love-dialog (see below). Lisette tells Orazio that her father has promised her to the Captain. Orazio is in despair. Malizia reassures him and promises to assist in preventing the marriage. They are heartened.

[Love Dialog for *Scene Four:*
WOMAN: Who is it?
MAN: One who wants nothing but to serve you.
WOMAN: My adored idol.
MAN: My very kind lady, you favor me all the time.
WOMAN: Little, if you consider your merits.
MAN: The usual excesses of your kindness.
WOMAN: On the contrary. Poor tribute for what I owe you.

MAN: You already know that I am your servant and faithful lover.
WOMAN: And I will be always constant in reciprocating your love.
MAN: If the sun of your beautiful face . . .
WOMAN: If the splendor of your face . . .
BOTH OF THEM: . . . make me enjoy paradise on earth.
MAN: Thus, with faithful heart . . .
WOMAN: With my constant love . . .
MAN: . . . I will live happily.
WOMAN: . . . I will consider myself blessed.
MAN: If you offer me your right hand . . .
WOMAN: If you give me your trust . . .
MAN: . . . to this faithful servant . . .
WOMAN: . . . to this faithful maid . . .
MAN: . . . my heart will not be able to long for anything more.
WOMAN: . . . I will not be able to desire anything else.
MAN: Here it is, and I assure you . . .
WOMAN: Take it, and I promise you . . .
MAN: . . . I will never change my mind.
WOMAN: . . . I will always be constant.
MAN: But if destiny were opposed . . .
WOMAN: If fate were adverse . . .
BOTH: . . . rather than engage to another, I would go to my death!
MAN: How happy I am, my beloved.
WOMAN: How happy I am, my beloved.
MAN: I am completely happy.
WOMAN: My dear, I must go.
MAN: Then go, sweetheart.
WOMAN: Assured that you are faithful to me.
MAN: I will be faithful, my love, until death.
WOMAN: Then, stay. Farewell.
MAN: Go, my happy idol.
(*They exit.*)]

Scene Five: Roberto and the Captain.
Roberto tells the Captain that he is ready to conclude their recent agreement to marry his daughter. The Captain confesses that his daughter has just been injured in an accident and has lost the power to speak. Roberto replies that this is even preferable since a dumb wife is less gossipy than other wives. They leave in order to draw up a contract.

Scene Six: Pulcinella, alone.
Frustrated, Pulcinella enters (here he can show up without his stick and hat) and complains that the pest Malizia spoiled his speech. Pulcinella explains that he went to his master's farm but could not find the master. He decides to return again to the farm.

Scene Seven: Malizia, Gabba, and Tristizia.
Malizia, Gabba, and Tristizia have their *lazzo about each other's name* (L07). They complain about their masters. Gabba asks if any of them know a physician, who is needed to cure the Captain's daughter of her dumbness. In an aside, Malizia reveals that this might be an opportunity to avenge himself against Pulcinella by declaring Pulcinella a seasoned physician. Malizia then tells Gabba that he knows a great physician who wears a white sackcloth and always conceals his real skills. This physician is always alone, pretends to be clumsy and ridiculous in speech, and never admits his greatness unless he is soundly beaten; in this way, he has given wonderful treatments. Now, if they want this miracle-worker, he will deny that he is a doctor; but, after a thrashing, he will admit that he is a physician and cure the patient. Gabba and Tristizia are amazed at the physician's modesty. They thank Malizia and all go off looking for the physician.

Scene Eight: Orazio and Lelio.
Orazio complains that the old man, Roberto, has promised his daughter to the Captain. Lelio enters separately and complains that the Captain has promised his daughter to Roberto. Orazio and Lelio notice each other and embrace. They each explain their love problems and promise to help one another. They decide that they will need their servants in order to plan a strategy. They exit.

Scene Nine: Pulcinella, alone.
Offstage, Pulcinella sings this song:
  Leave the hunting, and fish.
  The hunter [*sic*], to catch anything,
  Wastes his time and wears out the hook and bait.
  If he is lucky, he catches a worthless fish.
After the song, Pulcinella repeats it on the stage.

Scene Ten: The same with Gabba and Tristizia.
Watching Pulcinella sing, Gabba and Tristizia are amazed. Pulcinella

tells himself that he is a collection of virtues. The servants whisper to each other that this must be the great physician. While Pulcinella is praising himself, Gabba and Tristizia surround him and deeply bow. They have their *silent lazzi of putting on and taking off their hats* (I20). This is repeated three times. Then Pulcinella suggests that they leave on their hats lest they catch cold. Aside, the servants marvel that he really is a physician since he knows about colds. They move closer to Pulcinella. He shouts that they should keep their distance. They remark that it is a shame that a man of his qualities should hide his own virtues. Pulcinella has his *lazzi of searching his pants and pockets* (I18). After which, Pulcinella announces that he is not hiding anything. They speak of his great virtue in medicine. Pulcinella has his different laughes. They ask him to come cure the Captain's daughter. Pulcinella has his laughes again. He asks them if they have had lunch in reply to their questions (I19). This *lazzo* is repeated three times. One of them goes to get sticks. The servants apologize for being so rude. Pulcinella has his laughes. Then the servants beat him, while asking if he is a physician. He shouts yes and then denies it. This *lazzo* (D16) is repeated three times. Pulcinella pleads that he does not yet want to go to hell and begs them to stop. Finally he admits that he is a physician. The servants then want to dress him like "one of his peers." Pulcinella maintains that he already is dressed like one of his peers. The servants raise their sticks, and Pulcinella replies that if the devil wants this way, so be it. They all go and laugh on the way out.

ACT TWO

Scene One: Roberto and Lisetta.
Roberto, the old man, tells his daughter that he has promised her to the Captain. She replies that for the time being she does not want to marry. He rebukes her, insisting that she obey her father. She says that she is master of her own actions, and leaves. Roberto mutters that it's better to have raised a male pig that could be sold, than a useless sow. He exits, angry.

Scene Two: Lelio and Gabba.
Lelio speaks to Gabba of his love for Lesbia, the Captain's daughter. She has pretended that her powers of speech are lost in order to avoid marrying old man Roberto. But still Roberto has insisted on marrying her. Gabba promises to help Lelio, and they leave to plan a scheme.

Scene Three: Pulcinella, Tristizia, and the Captain.
Dressed as a physician, Pulcinella has his *lazzi of senseless Latin* (like
L12). Tristizia, his servant, explains to the Captain that this is a great
physician. The Captain bows to Pulcinella, and Pulcinella has his *lazzo of
"Put on Your Hat!"* (D15). The Captain explains that his daughter is sick.
Pulcinella feels the Captain's pulse. The Captain recoils; he is well, it is
his daughter who is ill. Treating the Captain like an ignoramus,
Pulcinella explains that by feeling the father's pulse, he can diagnose the
daughter's illness. The Captain and his servant are amazed, and quickly
praise Pulcinella's virtues. Pulcinella replies that the physician's art is really quite simple, and he could make the Captain a good physician. The
Captain says that it is not possible. Pulcinella picks up a stick and begins
to beat the Captain, causing him to run away. Tristizia reassures his
master that Pulcinella is a great miracle-maker. Finally, the Captain in-
vites Pulcinella into his house to cure his daughter. Pulcinella says that he
is ready, but first wants his fee. The Captain becomes confused. Tristizia
explains that Pulcinella wants money. The Captain pays Pulcinella, who
accepts the coins with his back turned, saying, "These things are worthless." To the audience, Pulcinella remarks that being a physician pays
better than being a farmer. They all go into the house.

Scene Four: Orazio, Malizia, and Lisetta.
Orazio tells Malizia that he wants to speak with Lisetta. Malizia knocks at
her door. Lisetta comes out and has a love scene with Orazio. Lisetta tells
Orazio that she does not want to marry the Captain, and Orazio asks
Malizia to mix the marriage up. The servant Malizia promises to do all he
can and pleads with them to leave lest Roberto discover their presence.
After they exit, Malizia wonders aloud how his Pulcinella scheme is work-
ing. At this point . . .

Scene Five: Malizia, Gabba, and Tristizia.
Malizia asks his comrades about the physician. Gabba praises him, saying
that he is now curing the Captain's daughter. The three decide to mix up
all the forthcoming weddings and go.

Scene Six: Pulcinella.
Entering, Pulcinella explains how easy it is for him to work as a physician,
especially since he was once a servant to one. This physician treated a
German once and wrote a prescription for him. Rolling the prescription

86

into a ball, the German ate it and was cured. Pulcinella concludes that
medicine is just the art of guessing, and so it will be for him. Pulcinella
dreams of becoming rich, buying land, riding in carriages. At this point
. . .

Scene Seven: Lelio and the same.
Lelio sees Pulcinella and bows to him. Pulcinella asks him to come closer
and attempts to feel his pulse. Lelio replies that he is well. Pulcinella asks
him, "Why do you come around looking for a doctor? When someone asks
for a chamber pot, that means he wants to shit. In the same way, when someone looks for a physician that means he is sick." Lelio explains he has a
different favor to request of Pulcinella; he knows that Pulcinella is
treating the Captain's daughter. Lelio would like to send her a message.
Pulcinella becomes angry, "What? A man like me, a protophysician, to
ask me to bring news? To be a pimp? A procurer?" Lelio tries to quiet
him. Pulcinella becomes angrier and angrier. This *lazzo* (B21) is repeated
three times. Eventually, Lelio takes out some money. Performing the *lazzo of behind the back*, Pulcinella takes the money, saying that he was only
kidding. Pulcinella, thanking Lelio, says he awaits Lelio's orders. Lelio
reveals his plan: he will dress as a physician and accompany Pulcinella to
Lesbia's room. Lelio promises to behave in a decent manner. Pulcinella
replies that he will have to put a harness on Lelio to make him behave
decently. Pulcinella says that he will even give Lelio a doctor's diploma
and picks up his stick. They leave, in good cheer, to dress Lelio.

ACT THREE

Scene One: Roberto.
Roberto decides to demand that his daughter, Lisetta, dress for her wed-
ding with the Captain, and he will marry Lesbia himself. He knocks on
Lisetta's door three times. Nobody answers. Then from her door.

Scene Two: Gabba and the same.
Gabba, coming out of Lisetta's room, starts to cry. He announces that
Lisetta has died. Roberto asks how it happened. Gabba explains that
Lisetta became depressed after Roberto rebuked her for not wanting to
marry the Captain and threw herself to her death. Sobbing, Gabba cannot continue to speak. Believing the story about his daughter, Roberto
laments that since she threw herself out of the window, her dress is now

dirty and he cannot return it. Gabba replies that she threw herself on the bed, then she got up and took a small decanter of poison, and then she threw herself . . . Gabba starts to cry. Roberto laments that if she took poison, then some must have spilled on the clothes and ruined them; so he still could not sell them back. Gabba explains that Lisetta threw the poison out the window, and began to cry and tear at her hair; she went into an apoplectic fit and . . . Roberto tries to conclude the story, "And then she died." No, Gabba replies, after two hours she recovered her senses, but suffered brain damage; she became mad and a physician is required. Roberto says that unnecessary expenses should be avoided. Gabba replies, "A physician is needed now." Roberto thinks that there is enough medication at home, but if Gabba can find a physician who charges no fee, then he is welcome. Gabba says he will find one. Going in the house, Roberto suddenly realizes if his daughter dies, he will have to pay for a funeral. Gabba has his *lazzi over his master's avarice.* He explains that Lisetta is well; his story was ruse to avoid marrying the Captain. At this point . . .

Scene Three: Orazio and Gabba.
Orazio sees Gabba and asks news of his sweetheart. Gabba tells of his trick. He helps dress Orazio as the free physician. Delighted, Orazio promises to pay Gabba back. They leave to complete their scheme.

Scene Four: Pulcinella and Lelio.
Pulcinella and Lelio, dressed as physicians, appear. Lelio wants to enter the Captain's house, but Pulcinella exhorts him to be wise, when . . .

Scene Five: The Captain and the same.
The Captain greets Pulcinella, saying he was searching for him. Pulcinella replies that he is ready to cure his daughter. When the Captain inquires who the second doctor is, Pulcinella informs him that this is his prize pupil, who specializes in difficult diseases. They all go in the Captain's house.

Scene Six: Malizia, Tristizia, and Gabba.
Delighted that their plots are working so well, Malizia, Tristizia, and Gabba speak of the tips they will receive from their masters, and how they will squander their earnings on their sweethearts and at the tavern. Gabba says they must all help Orazio, who is the most generous. They promise and go off to finish their schemes.

Scene Seven: Orazio.
Anxious, because he cannot find Gabba, Orazio calls for him.

Scene Eight: Gabba and Orazio.
Orazio asks Gabba what has transpired thus far. Gabba tells him about Lelio's doctor disguise. At this point . . .

Scene Nine: Pulcinella and the same.
Pulcinella comes out, saying, "*Ego sum merdicus, et de merdaccini disputabas.*" [Latin for: "I am a shitty man, and I will talk about shittiness."] Orazio, amazed that his servant-farmer is dressed like a physician, asks him how it came about. Pulcinella replies, "By force of beating, I received this privilege." If Orazio wishes to become a physician, Pulcinella explains, then Pulcinella will give him the same "privilege." Gabba realizes this will help with his plan. He threatens Pulcinella, saying that if he wants to avoid going to jail for misrepresentation, he must claim Orazio as a fellow physician. Pulcinella replies that it is fine with him. Orazio exits in order to dress as a doctor. At this point . . .

Scene Ten: Tristizia, Malizia, and the same.
Pulcinella claims he is confused with so many physicians walking around. Malizia makes fun of him. Pulcinella replies that when Malizia becomes sick, he will give him an enema of boiled water. Malizia swears at Pulcinella, who decides that he wants to change clothing and stop being a physician. Everyone threatens to beat Pulcinella, who goes upstage and says, "Since the devil wants it, I'll be a physician and a half." Malizia maintains that Pulcinella is no physician, just a peasant. Pulcinella denies that he wants to be a physician. This *lazzo* (D16) is repeated at least three times. They all exit with Pulcinella with their masters.

Scene Eleven: The Captain and Roberto.
The Captain praises the great virtue of the physician who is caring for his daughter; even his pupil is very learned. Roberto replies if he could get him for free then he would allow the physician to treat his daughter too. At this point . . .

Scene Twelve: Pulcinella, Lelio, Orazio, Gabba, and the same.
Lelio and Orazio are dressed as doctors. Gabba comes up to Roberto and explains that he has found an excellent physician. The Captain asks

whether it is the same person who is treating his daughter. Roberto asks Gabba, aside, whether this physician will work free of charge. Yes, Gabba answers, but since surgery is needed, it would be better to get one of the other doctors. Roberto calls for Pulcinella, who orders Orazio to treat the patient himself.

Scene Thirteen: Lisetta and the same.
Muttering crazy things and pretending she is mad, Lisetta enters. She walks to Orazio. Taking them aside, Pulcinella lectures the Captain and Roberto on medicine. Orazio announces to Roberto that it will be necessary for him to mimic marriage to his daughter in order to cure her. Roberto agrees, but Orazio must only *pretend* to marry Lisetta, just to quiet her. Orazio asks Lisetta if she wants him as her husband. She says yes. Both of the fathers smile; Orazio is just pretending. Orazio requests that Lisetta give him her hand, which she does. The fathers remark to each other that Orazio is very natural and plays his part very well. Lisetta asks her father for the dowry. Pulcinella tells old Roberto to play along, just to calm her. Roberto promises 5000 scudi. Orazio takes Lisetta's hand and they go off. The old men are astonished. Pulcinella reminds them that the lovers are just pretending and they act very naturally, very well. They all say to each other, "It's just a pretense." Then Lelio says he wants to treat the Captain's daughter, Lesbia, and enters the Captain's house. In the meanwhile, Pulcinella discusses the great virtue of medicine. Roberto asks what has happened with his daughter. Pulcinella explains that she is receiving very good treatment from the doctor: "The physician enters; the patient is up; the cockerel [Italian pun, also meaning simpleton] has been roasted; and he who knocks at the door is a cuckold." Roberto says, "But it's only a pretense!" Pulcinella reassures him, "Yes, it's only a pretense that the doctor has pretended to marry your daughter." The old men nod to each other, "It's only a pretense." At this point . . .

Scene Fourteen: Lelio, Lesbia, and the same.
Lelio takes Lesbia by the hand. Pulcinella explains, "This doctor too is pretending." Lelio announces, "This is not a time for pretense. I have married Lesbia." Incensed, the Captain goes wild, shouting and swinging. Orazio enters, quieting everyone, and announces that he has married Lisetta. The old men respond, "It was a pretense!" Orazio reveals that he is the real bridegroom; he is not a doctor but Orazio Alberigi, a man in love with Lisetta; he only pretended to be a physician in order to prevent

her marriage to the Captain. Roberto shouts that although he cannot un-do what has been done, the young couple will not receive any dowry or anything to pay for the wedding banquet. Orazio announces that he will do everything himself. Lelio says the same; they are happier this way. Everyone shouts, "Long live the physician by force!"

SELECTED BIBLIOGRAPHY

Beaumont, Cyril W. *The History of Harlequin.* 1926. Reprint. New York: Benjamin Blom, 1967.

Bragaglia, Anton Giulio. *Pulcinella.* Rome: Gherardo Casini Editore, 1953.

Disher, Maurice Willson. *Clowns and Pantomimes.* 1925. Reprint. New York: Benjamin Blom, 1968.

Duchartre, Pierre Louis. *The Italian Comedy.* Translated by Randolph T. Weaver. New York: The John Day Company, 1929.

Kennard, Joseph Spencer. *Masks and Marionettes.* New York: Macmillan Company, 1935.

Lea, K. M. *Italian Popular Comedy.* Two volumes. 1934. Reprint. New York: Russell & Russell, Inc., 1962.

McDowell, John H., "Some Pictorial Aspects of Early *Commedia dell'arte* Acting," *Studies in Philology,* vol. 39, no. 1 (January 1942), pp. 47–66.

Mic, Constant. *La Commedia Dell'Arte.* Paris: Editions de la Pléiade, 1927.

Nicolini, Fausto. *Vita di Arlecchino.* Milan: Ricciardi, 1958.

Nicoll, Allardyce. *Masks, Mimes and Miracles.* 1931. Reprint. New York: Cooper Square, 1963.

——————————. *The World of Harlequin.* London: Cambridge University Press, 1963.

Niklaus, Thelma. *Harlequin, or The Rise and Fall of a Bergamask Rogue.* New York: George Braziller, 1956.

Oreglia, Giacomo. *The Commedia dell'Arte.* New York: Hill and Wang, 1968.

Petraccone, Enzo. *La commedia dell'Arte—Storia, tecnia, scenari.* Naples, 1927.

Sand, Maurice. *The History of the Harlequinade.* Two volumes. 1862. Reprint. New York: Benjamin Blom, 1968.

Scherillo, Michele. "The Scenarios of Della Porta," *The Mask,* vol. 6, no. 1. (1913), pp. 33–48.

Schwartz, I. A. *The Commedia dell'arte and its Influence on French Comedy in the Seventeenth Century.* New York: Columbia, 1933.

92

Scott, Virginia P. "The *Jeu* and the *Rôle:* Analysis of the Appeals of the Italian Comedy in France in the Time of Arlequin-Dominique," in *Western Popular Theatre*. Edited by David Mayer and Kenneth Richards. London: Methuen and Company, 1977.

Smith, Winifred. *The Commedia Dell'Arte*. 1912. Reprint. New York: Benjamin Blom, 1964.

Thérault, Suzanne. *La Commedia dell'Arte*. Paris: Centre National de la Recherche Scientifique, 1965.